# THE CATHOLIC HOME

# The Catholic Home

BY
Father Alexander, OFM

Workingman's Publishing House
Costa Mesa, California

WORKINGMAN'S PUBLISHING HOUSE
360 East 15th Street, Costa Mesa, CA 92627
www.wphbooks.com
info@wphbooks.com
(949) 205-9736

The Catholic Home, by Father Alexander, OFM
This work is a faithful reprint of the original published in 1918 in England by R & T Washbourne, LTD

Designed and typeset by Seán R. Whittle

NIHIL OBSTAT:
    J. N. STRASSMAIER, SJ, *Censor Deputatus*
IMPRIMATUR:
    EDM. CANONICUS SURMONT, *Vicarius Generalis*

Westminster, 19 November 1917

NIHIL OBSTAT:
    F. ANDREAS EGAN, OFM, *Censor Deputatus*
IMPRIMATUR:
    F. FIDELIS CONDON, OFM, *Minister Provincialis*

London, 22 November 1917


Library of Congress Control Number: 2008929727
ISBN: 978-0-9818158-0-0


Printed in the United States of America

TO
THE MEMORY OF
MY PARENTS

# FOREWORD

THE Christian family is the unit which goes to build up the Catholic Church. To vary the metaphor, the Holy Family of Nazareth was the mustard-seed out of which the vast tree of the Universal Church has grown. In Joseph and Mary and the Holy Child we have the prototypes and models of the father, the mother, and the children who form the Catholic family. Indeed, it is the ideal of the family which pervades the whole constitution and life of the Church. Our Lord in His parables frequently refers to Almighty God as the Father of the family,* or simply as the Father. Think of the touching parable of the Prodigal Son. Christ taught us when we pray to address God as "Our Father." St. Paul tells us that after Him "all fatherhood in heaven and earth is named." † As Joseph, the foster-father, or legal father, of Christ in the home of Nazareth was, as spiritual writers tell us, the vicar or vicegerent of the Heavenly Father on earth—so that Mary could call him to her Divine Son, "Thy father" ‡—so do we

---

\* Latin *paterfamilias*
† Eph 3:15
‡ Lk 2:48

style the vicar or vicegerent of our Lord on earth, the visible head of His Church, the "Holy Father." And we love to speak of the Church herself as "Holy Mother Church," and are proud to call ourselves Her children. Everywhere the same analogy of the family life and relationship—father, mother, children.

The Christian family, then, is a very sacred thing. It is God's ordinary means for the salvation of souls. The Christian home is a shrine, an ark in which is preserved the priceless treasure of the Faith, and with it the virtues of the Christian life and heritage. Any book which makes us realize better these great truths; which teaches us love and reverence for the Christian family and home and home-life; which teaches parents the sublimity of their office in God's plans and raises up their thoughts to a higher conception of their privileges and duties; which teaches the adolescent the true sanctity and beauty of home, and, whilst filling them with a loving appreciation of what they owe to their parents, helps them to prepare themselves for the privileges and duties of Christian parenthood in God's good time—such a book is likely to produce very great good, not only spiritual, but even social, in these dark and deplorable days of materialism and the forgetfulness of man's higher destinies. But the little book before us seems to me to fulfill this task with a quite unusual measure of success. It handles great and often very delicate problems with theological clearness and sureness, combined with great reverence. It inspires an enthusiasm for the high, sacred ideals of family and home. I hope it will be very widely read by parents—especially by young parents—and by young married couples and youths and maidens who are preparing for the holy state of Matrimony. In these times, when so much pernicious teaching is widespread in literature and on the platform concerning the marriage tie and its obligations, it is well that the sane authoritative teaching of the Catholic Church should be clearly set before men's minds.

Sanctify the home and you will "renew the face of the earth" and regenerate a decadent world. May I, in conclusion, emphasize for Catholic parents, especially those just beginning the eventful journey of married life, one recommendation briefly touched upon by our author? I refer to the immense value of family prayer. Begin at least evening prayer, however short and simple, from the very first day that the new home comes into being; as God blesses you with children, train them up from their earliest years to join you in this beautiful Catholic practice, making yourselves little children and adapting your devotions to the simple minds of your little ones, developing them with their growth, physical and intellectual. Nothing will make a more profound impression upon them for their whole life, nothing will tend more to bless and sanctify your home and make it more and more like to the first Christian Home in Nazareth.

+ LOUIS CHARLES<br>
Bishop of Salford

November 29, 1917

# CONTENTS

**1** *Introductory* ○ 1
**2** *Looking Ahead* ○ 7
**3** *Reverence* ○ 13
**4** *Decay of Reverence* ○ 19
**5** *The Case for the Child* ○ 26
**6** *Home and School* ○ 33
**7** *Preparation for Marriage* ○ 43
**8** *Mixed Marriages* ○ 55
**9** *Husband and Wife* ○ 66
**10** *Parentage* ○ 75
**11** *Motherhood* ○ 84
**12** *Fatherhood* ○ 95
**13** *The Case for the Parents* ○ 104

# ONE
*Introductory*

ONLY when a cherished thing is in danger of perishing does its value appeal to the many. For the majority of men take their possessions and their successes and their pleasures as a matter of course. Only the few count the cost and justly appraise the value, for only the few think for themselves, and much thinking keeps them informed of the worth of what they have acquired or inherited. They look at it from all points of view; it becomes more or less identified with their lives; they view its possible loss with alarm; they strain every nerve to avert such a catastrophe. True, the sorrows of such men are greater than those of the thoughtless herd, for they apprehend more quickly and feel more keenly even the possibility of loss, but as their joys approach to ecstasy they can well afford to have them sobered by sorrow. They know that, here at least, the beauty of an object is brought into higher relief by attendant shadows: to stage a scene effectively the lights in the outer circle must be lowered. In heaven it may be different, but on earth the perfection of a picture depends not a little on light *and* shade.

For ever so long, thoughtful men have apprehended the loss of the home in the good old-fashioned sense: in the sense of its being the shrine of affection, peace, rest, stability and joy; in the sense of its being the foundation stone of the nation; in the sense of its being the hope—humanly speaking—of the Church, and one of the ante-rooms of heaven. The prospect has saddened them. Not for all the world would they wish to set back the hands of the clock, by throwing out of doors the social and domestic amenities that the passing years have brought with them, but they would fain wish to safeguard the privileges of home-life to the bitter end. Just as they wish the Englishman's house ever to be his castle, so do they wish their home ever to be the sanctuary of all the domestic virtues. So many and so grave have been the encroachments on the sacredness of the home, in recent years, that even the man in the street is waking up to the danger. God grant that there may be yet time to save it.

Those who, like the writer, can look back half a century will remember how the sapping and mining of home-life began and progressed. In the [eighteen-]sixties, tastes were simpler, wants were fewer, and outdoor attractions less numerous, exciting and alluring. The educational and recreative sides of life were by no means neglected, but their higher lights and their sweeter radiance were enjoyed more at home than abroad. Societies, confraternities, clubs, existed then as now; towns of any consequence at all had their lending libraries and reading rooms; there was no lack of theaters, and, in the season, excursions to beauty spots were the vogue, but there was no persistent and enticing lure from the home. The words of the old song found, in those days, a ready response in every heart: "Be it ever so humble, there's no place like home." *

With the [eighteen-]seventies, from many points of view, came remarkable changes. They set up music-halls, flooded the market with cheap and light literature, and sent giant bicycles careering far afield. The sapping and mining of attachment to the home had set in. From that period each decade has had its share in the work: witness the growth and variety of clubs and the ever-increasing fascination of club-life, the widespread facilities for traveling, the multiplication of places of amusement and picture-dromes, and the appeal made by the last-named even to children of tender age; the popularity of weekends; and, finally, the contemporary catastrophe which has sent so many members of the home warlike pilgrims over the globe, chained down so many others to late hours in munition works, and saddened the hearts of those too weak to work but keenly alive to mourning.

But it is just this last phase which may wake up the man in the street to the danger that lies at his door, that may save the home, as it is to be hoped it will save the nation. Thinkers, for a considerable time, saw that the nation was, on the one hand, lapsing into slumber, and, on the other, becoming dazed with pleasure. They tried, in vain, to wake it up and to warn. Whisperings were too gentle to be heard by a nation wearing the nightcap of self-content, warnings were regarded as too sanctimonious to

---

* *Home! Sweet Home!* by John Howard Payne

be heeded by a nation made dizzy with the whirl of pleasure.

Yes; whisperings were all too gentle—warnings were all too tender—it needed a war-alarm to rouse the slumberer; bombs were needed to sober the pleasure-seeker.

That men are wiser now is surely evident from their talk of what must needs be done when the nations have been sufficiently purged of their antagonism as to be able to sit round a table and discuss matters in sane and wholesome fashion: their blood-stained arms piled up in far-off corners, their numerous dead buried and wept over, and their women-folk and little children made happy in the hope of bright days that are to dawn. Who will not hope that those deliberations may be entered on with a sanity such as the world has not seen for ages past (for, surely, the Vicar of Christ will be allowed a voice)? Who will not pray that the peaceful efficacy of those deliberations may be testified to by the children's children of those now almost bled to death?*

We know not what will be the subject-matter of those contemplated debates, but who does not see that, if fundamental matters be overlooked, they will labor in vain who try to build anew? It would savor of pedantry to suggest that, at an international meeting, the home-life, as such, should be made a subject of debate; but as social reconstruction all round is sure to be the immediate outcome of those deliberations, we may take it for granted that later on, in the countries involved, steps will be taken to ameliorate the conditions of the home, if for nothing else than with a view to make good the indescribable loss of

---

* Written in the winter of 1917.

man-power in the present cataclysm. And surely it must be admitted that the home is the very foundation on which every nation rests. Granted that hostile artillery batter down every stately edifice, that liquid fire consume the literary treasures of all past ages, that poisonous gases reduce the earth to a barren waste, that fleets swept from the seas; *"the nation that rests on the foundation of family life has within itself an ever-renewed foundation of recovery."* *

This truth has, undoubtedly, been learned in the agonizing throes of the past few years. Antecedently to the [first World] War, the foundations of the home were being undermined, as we have partially seen; its pillars were tottering; husbands and fathers but too often regarded the home as a mere place of lodging, wives and mothers were becoming more and more impatient of their burdens, children were growing more impatient of control, and, as with the home, so with the nation—it was slowly drifting towards the lee-shore of effeteness. The nation can emerge from the furnace of affliction, purified, rejuvenated and strengthened, only by recognizing the innate value of the home. All must unite in restoring it to its honored place.

This cannot be done unless men think on right lines. If we are to judge by results, the thoughts of men have, for some generations past, slipped off those lines. To get back to them is a matter of urgent need, and hence the importance of having some of the cardinal points regarding home-life restated. For such a theme the times are surely ripe. That very convulsion which has hurled men leagues away from home, separated husband from wife, orphaned hundreds and thousands of children, expatriated and

---

* *Key to the World's Progress*, by Charles Stanton Devas, p. 109

interned numberless civilians, has had a most providential reaction in tightening the cords that bind heart to heart and soul to soul in the home. The roof-tree may have been burned down, the hearth may have been ground to powder, but, phoenix-like, the home will rise again and be more worthy of its name than it was before.

The present work is a humble attempt towards reconstruction. It does not pretend to be exhaustive. Its purpose will be served if it leads married folks to rise to the level of their responsibilities and if it induces our marriageable young men and women to approach the Sacrament of Matrimony with the necessary dispositions.

# TWO
*Looking Ahead*

IF, during our limited span here below, we wish to do practical work we must take the world as it is. In our particular sphere, our energies had better be used in striving to leave it a little better than we found it, rather than in attempting an upheaval of existing things. The old saying has it that a bad workman always quarrels with his tools, and many good people make themselves miserable and injure the cause they have at heart by their chronic dislike of everybody and everything around them. They seem to find a morbid delight in being out of touch with the times, strangely blind to the fact that the first imperative need of a would-be reformer is to be keenly alive to realities and that in every reality there must somehow and somewhere be a grain of good. The great thing is to find it. Were a lifetime spent in the search it would be well worthwhile.

Many regret the passing away of the "good old days," grow eloquent about the Ages of Faith, sigh for the dawn of better times, and all the while the sun rises and sets on days that are simply wasted in inanity; and the mourners sink into their graves and are forgotten, because of their leaving no trace at all, on the world's crust, of their existence. Indeed, from useful points of view, they might never have existed. "He that observes the wind shall not sow, and he that considers the clouds shall never reap." "Cast thy bread upon the running waters, for after a long time thou shalt find it again." \*

Nowhere, perhaps, is this more evident than in matters connected with the home. We find parents either wringing their hands or holding them helplessly by their sides; regretting that, owing to the changed conditions of life, they have no control over their children, or that, because of the reputed efficiency of teachers, authority is taken out of their hands, or, again, that the unsympathetic or arrogant spirit of the world renders all attempts at home-training useless in the extreme. "What's the use of training at home when it will surely and speedily be undone once the little ones have to face the wicked world?" Such parents forget that, *in all ages*, a wicked world had to be faced. "Love not the world, nor the things which are in the world ... for all that is in the world is the concupiscence of the flesh, and the concupiscence of the eyes, and the pride of life, which is not of the Father, but is of the world." † So, not only in the twentieth, but in the *first* century of Christianity, the world was regarded as the enemy of the home-bred child.

But let it be granted that life is not what it was. Life is what it is, and, being what it is, the great thing is to make the most of it, by using the passing hours to the best advantage. I once knew a man who boasted that he lived in

---

\* Eccles 11:4, 11:1
† I Jn 2:15, 16

the past and the future, for he regarded the present as altogether too materialized. He was not an idler by any means, but his pedantic view paralyzed his usefulness. He was regarded as a crank and died unregretted.

Parents must take life, with its facts, as they find it and provide strenuously against the dangers of the future, for it may be taken for granted that the lure from home will be even more pronounced in years to come than during the past few decades. The present [World] War will whet the appetite of youth for strange scenes and for new and exciting experiences. Trade unionism will eventually turn the whole world into one vast polyglot city. The foundations of the home should, therefore, be so propped up as to make it safe against all adverse floods. In the future, as in the past, it should have such a magnetic influence on those who go forth from it as to save them from danger when far away and loom up as a Mecca to which they would fain return at last to die. Home-builders should concentrate their energies on the equipment of their children for the new conditions of life. Those conditions will become more and more unfavorable to the conservatism of the home in the old-fashioned sense. If my boat is to be launched into the deep, I must first prove its seaworthiness. If wise, I wait not until it finds itself amidst possible breakers. Granted, then, that there are tempestuous waves on the sea of life that threaten to wreck, and strong currents that sheer off from the home-port, it behooves those responsible for the launching of children on the waters to look to it that charts are prepared and the home-charm so developed as to counteract all adverse agencies. It can be done. It must be done, for in God's providence, as we have said before, the home is the foundation of the nation, the hope of the

Church, the ante-room of heaven. Parents must not allow the customs of the world to dominate. Customs *will* exist, but they must be trained to creep around principles for their support rather than allowed to suffocate them. Where those customs are inherently evil, the well-trained child will know how to prune them; where they are good, they will help to strengthen the good principles imbibed.

All this suggests deeper consideration than is usual on the part of those responsible for the laying down of home foundations. Many young people contract matrimony without giving a single thought to the future; many in the married state leave all to priests and teachers, but, though priests may guide and teachers may help, the real responsibility for the well-being of the home rests on the shoulders of the parents, or the would-be parents. I say advisedly "the would-be parents," for just as the children should not be sent adrift without an adequate equipment of moral and social principles, so neither should men and women undertake the creation of a home without understanding what they are about. It is almost a crime to put off the consideration of such vital matters until the little ones are actually on the scene. In no other order of things is there such odious neglect and ignorance, neither is there in any other department of life such criminal waste. Thousands of lives are immolated yearly, and hundreds of thousands of souls are almost foreordained to damnation, because of the deplorable ignorance of marriageable people regarding the holy state that they contemplate entering. It seems to be regarded on the one hand as a huge joke, and on the other as a something that must be spoken of with bated breath. Shame! "This is a great sacrament, but I speak in Christ and in the Church." *

Nay, I should say that *all* adult lovers of the Church, the Empire and the race should have an intelligent understanding of the principles on which home-life is based, for there exists a large class who sit on the fence entirely out of sympathy with the home and void of reverence for the married state, who, nevertheless, dogmatize most fiercely about the numerical strength of families, domestic ties and duties, education and kindred matters, out of the profound depths of their ignorance. Some of them are too "refined" to dream of such a state for themselves, others are far too "religious" to study what they term an "indelicate matter," and all of them are too benighted to grasp the beauty and dignity of a state that God has made holy in the extreme by raising it to the dignity of a sacrament. They seem to forget that they themselves are the products—dare we not say, the *ungrateful* and *unworthy* products?—of matrimonial union, that they had homes, that the nation is a conglomeration of homes, and that, short of good homes, the Church cannot fulfill her divine mission. Judicious and timely knowledge would deepen their reverence, increase their helpfulness and eliminate their selfishness. It would, moreover, in divers cases, preserve the world from the fruits of the gross ineptitude shown by such people when they *do* (as sometimes happens) enter the holy state, for of all the uncanny things on the earth that surely is the most uncanny, i.e., entrance into a sacred contract of whose conditions the contracting parties are willfully ignorant because of a prudery which is wrongly styled innocence.

---

* Eph 5:32

And so these chapters should appeal not only to those who have homes or who mean, under God, to found homes, but also to those whose vocation may be in quite another direction. For it is occasionally members of this last-mentioned class who are the most prone to embarrass married people by their views, and the more ignorant they are the more insistent are they in proffering advice.

Much confusion of thought arises from regarding this as a sex-question and therefore one to be avoided. This is a great mistake. It is a much wider question. It is a fundamental question for the Christian, the Empire-builder and the lover of the human race, and, this being so, surely it needs no apology for treatment.

# THREE

*Reverence*

SOME folk smile when the story of Adam and Eve is retold. And they wish us to read into the smile, if not utter reprobation of that pathetic story, at least such distaste for it as grown-up people pretend for fairy-tales. They would have us believe that they have outgrown all that. They think it should end with the nursery, and that it is unfair to their intelligence for preachers and teachers to take it seriously and for writers to appeal to it. But there it is, and there it must remain. It has held the field for a long time, and wiseacres will be puzzled to suggest a more appealing and satisfying explanation of the beginnings of the home. For the home is the center and source—humanly speaking—of dominion, the nursery of the human race; the sanctuary wherein God means His attributes of wisdom, justice, love and mercy to be reflected; the one spot on earth whereon fidelity is legitimately symbolized by the most intimate of all human ties. Short of the reverent contemplation of the creation of that first couple, of the far-reaching commission given them, and of the marital powers imparted, no one can grasp the dignity of the home, nor can he frame laws for its preservation, or fashion a pathway fitted to lead to a satisfying goal. Apelike, his views of the home will be of the earth, earthly. His soul, meant to soar aloft, will be like to a man in a captive balloon, elevated, it may be, and, with wits sharpened and vision widened, able to scan his earthly brothers, but having no eyes at all for the greater realities beyond and above the clouds.

How mean and hide-bound such a man appears as the stupendous words of Genesis reverberate in our ears! Rolling over the wide expanse of nature, like ever-increasing peals of thunder, the ideas they convey are so many lightning shafts illuminating the rapt upraised countenances of believers, and revealing the would-be descendants of apes scuttling off for shelter in the brushwood. How potently those words remind us of the glory of our origin and of the power given to man in the first home of Eden, "Let Us make man to Our image and likeness, and let him have dominion over the fishes of the sea, and the fowls of the air, and the beasts, and the whole earth, and every creeping creature that moves upon the earth." * How modestly the idea of sex is conveyed, and how purposeful its meaning in the case of those destined to found homes: *fruitfulness* to be regarded as their special blessing and *indissolubility* to be the natural outcome of matrimonial consummation, as was, later on, made clear by our Blessed Lord, "Wherefore now they are not two, but one flesh. What, therefore, God has joined together, let no man put asunder." † "And God created man to His own image; to

---

\* Gn 1:26
† Mt 19:6

the image of God He created him; male and female He created them. And God blessed them, saying, 'Increase and multiply, and fill the earth and subdue it, and rule over the fishes of the sea, and the fowls of the air, and all living creatures that move upon the earth.'" * "And the Lord God built the rib which He took from Adam into a woman, and brought her to Adam. And Adam said, 'This now is bone of my bones, and flesh of my flesh; she shall be called woman, because she was taken out of man.' Wherefore a man shall leave father and mother, and shall cleave to his wife, and they shall be two in one flesh." †

Who can read these words with reverential mind without finding his heart beat faster and his soul lifted up in praise of the great Creator on the one hand, and, on the other, without being filled with admiration of the first couple whose marriage was assisted at by the whole court of heaven, and who obtained at first hand the blessing of God Himself? Who does not feel a pang in knowing that their felicity was so short-lived, and who will not profit by the reflection that its transitoriness was due to the breach of a divine command? True, in the very hour of condemnation, mercy was measured out with no niggard hand, but the woes that nevertheless have followed should long ere this have warned all who build homes of the danger of incurring God's displeasure by disregard of the lines on which the foundations should be laid, for "unless the Lord build the house, they labor in vain that build it." ‡

---

\* Gn 1:27, 28
† Gn 2:22-24
‡ Ps 126:1

Never, in the whole course of history, did beginnings seem so full of promise. All Heaven contemplated with satisfaction the new departure: a couple created in the state of perfect nature, constituted in grace, endowed with preternatural gifts, intellectually equipped beyond all powers of description, physically perfect, yet falling so low because of lack of co-operation with the known will of God. How Heaven must have wept! How Hell must have exulted! How the earth, since then, has groaned! How would-be heads of families should take to heart the time-honored lesson!

Have not we, therefore, sufficient warrant for harking back to that first marriage? Had it merited the continued blessing of God, so generously bestowed, how different would have been the state of the human race. Is it not, then, clear that the earth can be brought back to, at least, a semblance of its original state only by looking well to home foundations? Fair may be the woman, naturally gifted may be the man, but unless both bring to the marriage state hearts and souls pleasing to God, and intentions squaring with His divine laws, all their efforts at home-building, in the Christian sense, will be in vain. The story of Adam and Eve is for all time. The bitter experiences of Adam and Eve are object-lessons for all called to their state of life.

The first truth that must be grasped by would-be parents is that "Matrimony is a holy state, originally instituted by Almighty God between our first parents, ratified and confirmed by Jesus Christ, honoured by His first miracle and raised to the dignity of a *Sacrament,* as a *most holy sign* and mysterious representation of the indissoluble union of

Christ and His Church." [*] They are to remember that God in His goodness, through this holy sacrament, blesses them with sanctifying grace to enable them to love one another, to restrain concupiscence, to bear with each other's weaknesses, to help each other to attain the end for which they were created and to bring up their children (if blessed with such) in the love and fear of God, and that all these favors are *dependent on their entering into it and persevering therein in a holy manner and in having a right intention.*[†]

Were these fundamental truths grasped by the contracting parties *before marriage*, how different would be the state of society! Ignorance thereof crowds the marriage-market with persons void of a spark of reverence for this great sacrament, and without reverence the contract of matrimony becomes but a glorified state of "White Slavery." To induce reverence, something must appeal to the *soul*. Beauty may inspire admiration, strength may beget trust, nobility of character may induce a species of nature-worship, thrift may secure comfort, but only the contemplation of the divine in matrimony can conjure up the reverence due to it, and without reverence it would be almost brutish and could never be entered into with a feeling of individual or mutual respect.

How it is redolent of the divine! Home is the laboratory in which the Creator—when He so wills—turns out His masterpieces in the shape of lovely children, through the co-operation of the parents; it is the stage on which He displays His adorable attributes—providence, love, wisdom and compassion—more perhaps than anywhere else

---

[*] *Old English Ritual*
[†] *ibid.*

in the wide world; it is the preparatory school for all the world's work; the training college, in embryo, for Church Councils and for National Parliaments, and it is the sanctuary wherein the saints of God first receive the precepts which, reduced to practice later on in life, raise them to the honor of the altar and to His Kingdom above. Almost thirty years ago I remember the present Bishop of Salford stating, in a lecture, that all the saints (with the exception of St. Wenceslaus[*]) had saintly mothers, which was tantamount to saying that all the saints had good homes, for, as we shall see in a future chapter, it is the mother who, most of all, makes the home. Without the note of reverence being struck, good homes must ever remain an idle dream and our young people, preparing for matrimony, cannot hear that note if they listen only to worldly clamor. The crude, erotic, emotional or mercenary notes struck by the world will so dull their sense of hearing as to drown the refined, matured and elevated notes of God's mouthpiece—the Church. The dominant note is, as I have said, *reverence*: reverence for God the Creator, reverence for matrimony as a sacrament, reverence for each other, and, finally, reverence for its fruits—the earthly angels lent to loving parents by God, when He deigns to bless the marriage with fertility, in order that they may first of all, gladden the earthly home; gladden, in after years, the world; and, in eternity, gladden the heaven which that same God means to be their *true* and *lasting home*.

---

[*] St. Wenceslaus was reared by his grandmother, a holy woman, whose home was good.

# FOUR
*Decay of Reverence*

MOST students of social life are of opinion that, in the modern world, reverence is on the wane. If this be granted, a question at once arises as to the part, if any, played by the home in the alleged failure.

In the preceding chapter we pleaded for reverence on the part of those who felt called upon to found a home—reverence for the holy state of matrimony, mutual reverence, and reverence for their offspring—and so, on this ground alone, we are committed to an inquiry as to whether the alleged decay of reverence is traceable to the shrine in which the citizens of the world receive their first impressions. That shrine, as we have more than once said, is the home.

Now it may be taken as an axiom that goodness, to be imitated by the young, must first be seen; for children are nothing if not imitative. And, as goodness inspires reverence, it follows that, if the home influence be good, reverence on the part of the children will, as a rule, keep pace with it. But before going further, let us be quite clear as to what we mean by reverence. We mean by it a feeling of profound respect (often mingled with awe and affection), which, in its higher development, may assume the form of veneration and adoration. McCosh, in his notable work on emotions,[*] distinguishes several stages on the way to reverence. First of all, one is struck with what either really is or is supposed to be great in power, intellect, or goodness, and anticipates the salutary effects that are to follow; then admiration, wonder and reverence are excited, and when the objects contemplated are good, these qualities belong to the moral order. So deep may be the impression made, that veneration may be induced, especially for the aged, the ancient, and the grand. Inquisitiveness, therefore, is of the greatest possible value in the education of the child, for, if properly directed, it leads to reverence and awe, and enters largely into the adoration and worship of God.

What has just been said may be thus simplified, so as to bring it into line with ordinary forms of speech. Reverence means a feeling of *deep respect*. Now, seeing that *ordinary* respect means a just regard for, and appreciation of, excellence—especially moral worth—whether that of persons or things; conformity in the heart or conduct to duty or obligation; regard for law, and deference to whom deference is due, it follows that *deep respect*, i.e., *reverence*, means much more.

Who does not see that, if parents rightly fulfill the duties of their state, reverence on the part of the children will follow as a matter of course? But those duties cannot be rightly fulfilled unless the parents themselves approach them in a reverential spirit. The stages on the way are

---

[*] *The Emotions*, by James McCosh, p. 139

similar to those on the child's way to reverence: wonder, admiration, awe, and (possibly) veneration; wonder at the inscrutable ways of God in choosing them to contribute to the citizenship of heaven, by, first of all, selecting them to bring citizens into the world; admiration of the little ones who, of a surety, until the age of reason, retain their baptismal innocence; awe in conjuring up the child's future career; reverence even for the body of the child because of its being the shrine of an immortal soul, and veneration for that soul whose infusion is altogether outside of their power, but is the outcome of the direct creative work of God. Filled with this spirit of reverence how anxiously the parents will strive to lead sober, just, prudent, charitable and religious lives, knowing as they do that in no other way can reverence be built up in their offspring.

It is, surely, widely known that God, in the soul of the child, has provided a fertile field for the cultivation of this spirit of reverence. If the little one leaves the home, on its godmother's arm, as a child of nature, he returns to it, from the Font, as an adoptive child of the Heavenly Father: an heir, according to hope, of everlasting life; a member of the Church and with a soul full of sanctifying grace. At or after the age of reason he may deliberately surrender his birthright, but until then it is true to say that the child is as pure as any angel. As an educational writer[*] wisely says, "The first six years of a child's life are of inestimable importance." Thus splendidly equipped, the child comes into the world as a little pilgrim on his way to his Heavenly Father's house, and Jesus Christ hurls woes on the heads of those who would dare impede his progress: "But he that

---

[*] Dr. Maria Montessori

shall scandalize one of these little ones that believe in Me, it were better for him that a millstone should be hanged about his neck, and that he should be drowned in the depth of the sea." *

These words are the child's charter of rights: a right to have his body cared for, inasmuch as it is the tenement of the soul; a right to have the powers of the soul cultivated, for the soul was redeemed with Christ's Precious Blood; a right to have what is popularly called "a chance in life," for the earth is the Lord's and the fullness thereof, and the child, being the child of the Lord, has a right to share in its fruits. Be he the child of a pauper or the heir to a throne, it is all the same: he must be allowed a fair field for the exercise of all his Heaven-given faculties and must be left free to get to God by the pathway traced by Him who founded the One True Church; otherwise he is scandalously and criminally wronged.

Apart from the supernatural endowments above referred to, we find in the child a marvelous instinct that betrays itself in a hundred ways, sometimes to the embarrassment and, at other times, to the annoyance of those who have no particular sympathy with child-life in its earlier stages. It is the instinct of wonderment. It is seen in the eyes, wide open, that fix you and follow all your movements, and are said to cover an evil-minded man with confusion; it is manifest in the dartings and gropings of the little line-covered hands, so eager to have and to hold, and in the keen apprehension of varying light and sound and movement. The child actually revels in wonderland.

---

* Mt 18:6

Now, as we have already seen, wonder is the first step towards reverence, and the child, as it develops, is naturally inclined to take all the steps until it reaches the goal. His father looms up before him as an embodiment of strength and a model of rectitude. When apprehensive of danger, he clutches his hand and fears not; in moments of doubt he feels that father's way must be the right way, and, so, in following it, he falters not. His mother is his queen. She may be poor, illiterate, slattern and dowdy in her dress; but as the child knows not yet the real or conventional value of wealth, education, deportment and fashion, no other woman, be she even a duchess, can get between him and the woman at whose bosom he was nursed and by whose knee he learnt his first lessons, rude as they may have been. He reveres her; instinctively, he is awe struck in her presence.

Is not this child's soul, then, a most fertile field for parental labor? Do we not realize that if, in the first six years of a child's life that field be thoughtfully cultivated, the fruits, as a rule, will be as lasting as they are abundant? And the most precious of all those fruits will be reverence; deep respect for parents and for all others exercising authority, appreciation of and admiration for goodness; awe in the presence of the noble and the grand; veneration and adoration of Almighty God, the Supreme Good.

Let it not be imagined that our enthusiasm has carried us into the land of dreams and that we are picturing an impossible child. Far from it. We are perfectly aware of the child's limitations, for, although sanctifying grace is still in his soul, he is nevertheless a child of fallen nature, and many indeed are the traces thereof, shown even in his early years. The uninitiated (especially those intellectual freaks who worship poodles and disdain the "mere child") put down those exhibitions of fallen nature as most shocking irreverences, but the initiated have a clearer vision. The initiated are those who try to see things in God's perspective: with the eyes of *faith* as well as reason. They know that all the pranks of the child enter into the making of the future man. He has other instincts besides wonderment and he is bursting with physical activities. If those instincts be fettered and if his activities be repressed, he may develop into a living mummy, but he can never grow up into a man of character. He is inquisitive and venturesome: eager to dissect the interiors of his toys and to find out whether the fire on the other side of the screen really burns; he soils his clothes and ruthlessly rends them; robs bird's nests and paddles ankle-deep in slush, regardless of boot-polish and knitted socks; he climbs over wire-entangled fences and swings on spiked gates; is chummy with every dog he meets but is death on cats; he is pushful, boisterous and sometimes greedy, but on most occasions he offers his apple that another may have the first bite; he is pugnacious at one moment, cowardly at another, occasionally mean, but most times generous and unselfish; he has a keen sense of the abnormal, the ridiculous, the unusual—call it what you will—and, so, laughs at the odd and the eccentric, although the place may sometimes be sacred and the person may be a great dignitary; but it is, precisely, with all the abandon, freshness and innocence with which he explodes with laughter at the clown in the circus. In all this there is neither irreverence, nor cruelty, nor malice; there is simply the exuberance of high spirits and the unconscious exercise of the splendid physical and mental powers with which God has blessed him. Looked at in the right way they are simply delightful, for they give assured promise of good things to come if, happily, instead of being sternly and cruelly repressed, they be directed into healthy channels. They are perfectly compatible with deep-seated reverence provided that, with the flight of years, an appeal be made to his head as it was made, in infant years, to his heart. God lodged the instinct of reverence in his heart; it is for the parents to keep it lodged there, by putting the idea of reverence into his head. If the head be forced to dislodge reverence from the heart, through the discovery of glaring imperfections in the parents, then the poor child is being robbed of his rights. He has a right to be shown good example. If it be not shown, an occasion is presented for wrong-doing, and the first real wrong-doing on the part of a child is usually the result of loss of reverence for those who were hitherto regarded as his idols. So long as they kept to their pedestal, by faithful fulfillment of their duty, the child's respect was assured. When they descended, through the perpetration of some flagrant inconsistency, that respect was lost, and the child was found muttering his first *"I don't care!"*

Would that it ended with that, but, alas! it is to be feared that much of the irreverence that moralists speak of is traceable to the home. More's the pity, for, in the light of what we have said, it should not be so. The child should leave the home brimful of reverence for the good, the true and the beautiful. If he leaves it otherwise, he is badly equipped for his struggles in the wide world. There the citadel of reverence is sure to be assailed, but, oh, what sacrilege to have it destroyed before he leave the home at all.

# FIVE

*The Case for the Child*

WE have seen that the child comes from the hands of God gifted with a wonderful instinct of reverence. For a considerable time his sphere is a limited one—confined, for the most part, to the home, the school and the playground—yet, even in that limited sphere, he comes in contact with others who, spiritually and socially, may excel his parents. They fail, however, to dislodge father and mother from the position they have taken up in his mind and heart. The priest visits the school and is at once awe-inspiring and kindly; the kindergarten mistress does her work with as much motherliness as precision; his relatives may be, materially speaking, even more indulgent than his parents; but all those forces make on the child but passing impressions. His parents continue to hold the field in his affections: the father is still, to him, a tower of strength; the mother retains her position as a model to be admired and imitated.

This incomparable instinct serves its divinely intended purpose up to the age of reason. If, after that age, there be solid ground for assent, then what was formerly a mere instinct is adopted by the reason and made its own. Reverence, as a natural consequence, will grow apace. The reverence that, all unconsciously, was exercised on trust will now rest on such solid ground as to be able to withstand all reasoning to the contrary.

Hitherto, reverence was instinctively based on the strength of the father and the loving tenderness of the mother. After the age of reason something more is needed if it is to retain its hold on the child. In school he is now being trained to exercise his powers of observation, comparison and expression. Not a single word escapes his keen ear, not a thing is done without its appeal to his notice. He has a tolerably clear sense of right and wrong, and if the right be suitably put before him—especially by his parents—he needs but gentle guidance to be induced to follow it.

From this it follows that if, after the age of reason, a high standard of conduct be not set up, and kept continually before the child's mind, reverence will be sure to dwindle. So far, reverence has not been subjected to any particular test; but now that the child is capable of *exercising* his reason, one of his first impulses will be to apply tests. In other words, the child will be critical. If the standard of conduct at home is, at least, as high as that of the school; if the parents are as truthful, just, kind and orderly as the child's teachers; if they are respectful to the clergy and faithful to their religious duties; then the reverence that was instinctively imbibed and that, largely, was God's gift, will now be deepened. While remaining a precious gift of God it will, nevertheless, become meritorious on the part of the child, and will influence his whole career. Later on in life he may, happily, come in contact with holy, refined and highly educated people, but, exalted though they be, they will add nothing to his store of reverence: that store was laid up in the old home. When he leaves that home his life is spent in paying easy reverence to authority, high principle and general worth, wherever he finds them. Every new act of reverence but intensifies the value of the original gift and makes him more keenly alive to any departure from the standards that he was trained to revere. Need it be said that it is on such foundation the welfare of the world rests?

We find this verified in really Catholic countries, wherein great store is laid by home life. To go no farther than Catholic Ireland: what most strikes the intelligent observer is the atmosphere of reverence for all that is pure and noble. It illumines the brow of the little barefooted boy on the mountainside and adds new glory to the grey hairs of venerable men and women. Mere tourists are wont to put down this national trait to abjection and servility, but the student traces it to the fireside of even the meanest hovel where holiness of life, learning, unblemished pedigree, high principle and purity are extolled and set up as standards to be reached. Herein lies the secret. Reverence is the product of the home, and what is learnt at home is never forgotten.

When the critical spirit is awakened in the child, and he begins to apply tests to conduct, if he find that the old foundations of reverence have shifted, who can conceive the extent of the harm that is done? The poor child finds himself in a sad predicament. In school he is trained to piety, decency, diligence, order and cleanliness, and he learns to appreciate the importance of one and all. At home, alas! they are conspicuous by their absence. Priests and teachers influence him for good, but for a fraction of the twenty-four hours. The remainder of the day falls under the baneful influence of parents who are void of principle and utterly destitute of the domestic virtues. Seeing that the home is, after all, his natural refuge and that the parents are his natural protectors it follows that, in the mental combat which ensues, the home instinct of the child prevails. His reason shows him the right, but as the united forces at home are either opposed to it or indifferent, he ends by judging that the practice of right is impossible. Slowly but surely he becomes inoculated with the idea that right living is, doubtless, a splendid thing for those who live lives of ease, but is incompatible with the rough-and-tumble life to which he is accustomed, and from which he feels he cannot rise. Although he cannot but admire the healthier and holier atmosphere of church and school, yet, as he breathes an unwholesome atmosphere for the greater part of his child-life, his spirituality and mentality do not thrive and he begins life in the world most heavily handicapped. It seems to me that herein lies the root of the evil that is so often ascribed to the modern child, as if he alone were the culprit. I think he is, for the most part, unfairly treated. Had the necessary conditions of reverence been fulfilled, the child's pliable nature would have been brought into line with right principles and our ears would not be shocked, as they so often are nowadays, with the outcry about juvenile crime and depravity.

It may be objected that, later on, when freed from the baneful influences of home, true principles, learned in church and school, will reassert themselves, and that the balance of reverence for the good, the true and the beautiful will be restored. Although contemporary history proves the possibility of such an issue, yet it must ever remain the exception. Two or three notable men of today boast of having risen from lowly conditions of home life. All honor to them! But what are they among millions? In all time the child is father to the man, and so we must deal rather with rules than exceptions. If, therefore, the child at home is daily confronted with all that contributes to irreverence rather than to reverence, it follows that he will carry into the world the spirit in which he has been nurtured. If God has not been adored and worshipped in spirit and in truth by the parents; if prayer has been neglected; if the Sundays have not been kept holy; if the Friday abstinence has not been kept; if honesty, truth, decency, sobriety and order have been violated; if the priests of God have been treated with scant respect; if teachers have been belittled and contradicted; who does not see that the benighted child has been equipped—and by his own parents only—for the ranks of the decadent? Priestly lessons and advices will appear to him but so many impracticable burdens, his fallen nature will predispose him to glide down the path of least resistance; he will find it easier to do the wrong thing rather than the right; a certain undefinable irritability towards law and order will supervene, for these demand self-restraint, and self-restraint was the thing, above all, that least appealed to his parents. The child will face the world almost as the avowed enemy of everything that is orderly and right; he will be prone to resist established authority; in one word he will be irreverent.

His irreverence is the natural outcome of his parents failure to rise to the level of their responsibilities. Had they done so, their mutual reverence for the child would have developed, year by year, until he was fitted out for the world. Reverence on their part would have begotten reverence on his, and a thoroughly equipped unit would have been added to the Church and the nation. Parental reverence for the child leads them to regard him not as a mere wage-earner in the future, nor as a mere man of the world, but as, primarily, a child of God, a member of the One True Church and an heir of heaven. All mundane considerations must take a secondary place in the child's training. Duty to God and to Holy Church must come first. It must leaven all the actions of the day and must be the first and last court of appeal. Short of this being remembered and reduced to practice, the whole child is not educated as it ought to be. The natural side, if cultivated at all, will be over-cultivated, and the result in future years will be manifest in cynicism regarding holy things and all that savors of the supernatural. If this spirit abounds today, even amongst the young, it is to be feared that it was cradled in the home. Had the home been permeated with an atmosphere of reverence for God and holy things and persons, the evil influences of the world would not, so soon, have dispersed it.

Even well-disposed parents are far too prone to leave all such instruction to teachers in school and to the clergy. I am convinced that this is a cardinal error. If we conjure up memories of the past we shall find that the lessons best remembered are those learned by our fond mother's knee and sanctioned by the smiles of our father. Priests and teachers cannot supply for the lack of those early lessons. If the modern world is to be regenerated, the parents must have the patience to imitate those of previous generations by gathering their children around them, in their earlier years, and speaking to them of the things that matter: the Fatherhood of God, the childhood and Passion of our beloved Redeemer, the sanctity of our holy mother Mary, the existence and beauty of the angels, the beauty of virtue, and the ugliness of wrong-doing. For this noble task nothing more is wanted than the maternal instinct. Every true Catholic mother—trained by her own mother's knee—has the necessary dogmatic knowledge, and if she speaks as a mother she uses a tongue given neither to priests nor to teachers. *Their* tongues may reach the inner mind, but the mother's tongue reaches the profoundest depths of the heart—and a child has far more heart than mind.

If this most important of all domestic works be neglected, then school instruction will prove but a thin veneer that will soon rub off through contact with the materialistic world. For the *all-around* training of the child, for the perpetuity of the spirit of reverence, for the betterment of the world, the growth of religion and the glory of God, the parents must deepen their sense of responsibility by cultivating the spirit of reverence for the little ones confided to them by the Almighty Father. That sense of responsibility has but one form of expression, i.e., cultivation of the home virtues, and the exercise of patience and perseverance in instructing the children as if all depended on their own unaided efforts. *Then* there will be such splendid interaction as between home and school and church as will render fruitless all attacks from without.

# SIX
*Home and School*

WE have found that when parental reverence is wanting, the child is badly equipped for his struggles in this world and for his welfare in the next. The sense of responsibility induced by reverence restrains the parents from acting capriciously in the upbringing of their children. The more they take to heart the onerous nature of their obligations, the greater becomes their anxiety to find out and to be guided by true principles of education. Seeing, then, that those feelings of responsibility are based on the supernatural destiny of the child, it is but right that parents should look to the Church for guidance. They conceive that it is part of the mission of the Church to lay down safe rules of action in all matters of faith and morals. And, from the age of reason, the faith and morals of the child are at stake. Far from thinking that, in listening to the Church, they are yielding up their liberty, Catholic parents are aware that they are simply following the dictate of right reason. Amidst the clash of modern opinions on education, in which agnostic and undenominational views are, usually, the most clamorously voiced, they believe that the Church, which is the pillar and the ground of truth, will have something to say. They cannot bring themselves to think that the Church, which educated her children in spite of pagan Rome, and which combatted false philosophies for nineteen centuries, has, in the twentieth century, lost her voice.

If Catholic parents are of average intelligence and have used their talents as the Church is ever urging them to do, they will have arguments to hand to meet the objections of opponents who complain of ecclesiastical interference, and who talk glibly of the retrogressive spirit of the Church. Sad to say, some educationalists, who ought to be better informed, range themselves on the side of our most virulent antagonists. The parents above spoken of will point proudly to Catholic countries wherein children of the One True Church have been pioneers in science and art, music and literature. The non-Catholic artist has yet to be born who will put before our eyes such a picture of the Crucified as will move our hearts. Outside the Church no soul-inspiring Madonna has ever been put on canvas. No music can so thrill the heart with pure emotion as that of a Mass composed by a Catholic whose soul is uplifted by the reality and the sublimity of the Holy Sacrifice. Catholic scientists, from Roger Bacon to Pasteur and Secchi, have rendered glorious the ages in which they lived, and even now they are in the front rank. Library shelves groan under the contributions of Catholic authors to pure literature, and the Church that can boast of a Dante and a Francis Thompson has no need to bow its head in shame, in the presence of the most exacting critics. Before Columbus saw the light, and from his time even until now, navigators and explorers have not found their Catholicity a bar to intrepidity. And when rights have had to stand the test of fire and sword, the thumb-screw and the rack, who will dare say that our holy religion has ever yet turned men into cowards? All that is really sublime in the religious architecture of our own and of every other civilized country is the product of Catholic brains and the work of Catholic hands.

In a Protestant country like our own, where Catholics have been emancipated but for ninety years,* it is absolutely necessary to keep the foregoing facts before our minds. If we failed to do so, we might end by believing the oft-repeated charge that the Church is, either openly or in some occult way, the enemy of learning and the opponent of progress. By remembering what the Church has done, for the glory of God and the benefit of the world at large, parents will be stimulated to follow her splendid example, by setting up high standards of education for their children. The point to be borne in mind is that the Church which has been the patron (and occasionally the inspirer) of the arts and sciences, the warden of philosophy, and the creator of theology, could not possibly, after twenty centuries of constant exercise be oblivious, even for a generation, to the lawful and righteous wants of the times. The supposition has only to be mentioned to show its absurdity. This accounts for the readiness of the well-informed Catholic parent to embrace the suggestions of the Church with regard to what matters in education. He takes the shifty and ever-changing views of educationalists for what they are worth; he gives earnest thinkers their due, but, first and last, when he wants to know the principles

---

* 1829 is generally regarded as the decisive year for Catholic emancipation in the United Kingdom.

that should dominate true education, he looks to the teaching Church for guidance.

The Church tells him that, in home education, as has more than once been said, God must have the first place; the laws of the Church must be known and respected; the child must be instructed, corrected and be shown a good example. Thus, in brief, is the parent informed of his responsibilities and of his consequent duties. Thus his reverence is deepened. Thus the home is made contributory to the sanctification and general well-being of the child. Although the parent may be ignorant of the technicalities of education he will, if obedient to the Church, be really acting on the lines laid down by the most eminent modern educationalists. They tell us that "to educate means to bring up or lead forth the child. That is done by utilizing the life that is already there. Education is not imposed: it is conducted." But that the life "already there" may wax strong, the child, we may be allowed to add, must be furnished with suitable sustenance for soul, mind and body. The real meaning of education is to present that food in a manner best suited for assimilation so as to *help* and not to *force* the growth of soul and body. The Church is the sole arbiter as to what spiritual food is fit for her little ones, and she will never relinquish her right to have it doled out as she judges best. She is the Spouse of the Divine Teacher who said, "Suffer the little ones to come to Me, and forbid them not; for of such is the Kingdom of God." \* She must be faithful to Her mission.

The work of sanctification and general betterment of the child is extended and forwarded in the school. In

---

\* Mk 10:14

Catholicism, there is ever the closest possible connection between the two. This is a feature peculiar to Catholic life, and it accounts for the almost childlike reverence of traditional Catholic parents for the teacher. To them, he is a kind of second self; but a second self invested with almost sacerdotal dignity because of his exalted office. They know that his beliefs are identical with their own, and that his primary idea is to lead their children on, step by step, to God. They feel that, the higher his religious ideal, the more conscientious will be his school work. This fact, which holds good in all departments of activity, is especially prominent in the sphere of education. It is the teacher of high moral tone who makes the most lasting impression.

This connection of the Catholic home with the school renders it impossible to treat of the one without, at least, some reference to the other. It enables us to understand the meaning of what is called a "Catholic atmosphere," without which, we are all agreed, our schools cannot exist. No thoughtful Catholic can ever be content with a paltry thirty or fifty minutes per day for religious instruction. He conceives that the entire day must be pervaded with the Catholic spirit that exists in the home, so that, when the leaving age is reached, the child will go forth into the world equipped all round for his start in life. He has been aided in every way likely to insure success. From his infancy until the age of fourteen there has been absolute unity of aim between parents, priests and teachers. His future will depend largely on himself, but, as a fifth part of the average life of man has been passed in integrity, there is every likelihood that it will be difficult indeed to dislodge him from his position as a faithful child of God.

Even should he fail, he will have a much better chance of recovery than the boy whose early education was defective. Sooner or later it will dawn on him that the way of evil is illusory: that happiness does not depend on worldly success nor on sensual gratification, but rather on integrity and self-restraint. Fond memories of the simple virtuous home and of his school-life will revive; parents, priests and teachers will be recognized as his best friends; after, may be, many wanderings he will find his soul again, and, like the prodigal, he will return.

The youth, on the contrary, whose home training and education were deficient has no such anchor of hope to cling to in the hour of distress. His baser life, as the years glide on, differs only in degree from what it was in childhood. Memories of the old home do not lift him out of the sea of despair. His infancy and childhood saw him cast off from even natural moorings. He was nurtured in contempt of the supernatural and has never once rested foot on a spiritual islet. Tossed about from the crest of one wave of temptation to another, swallowed up in the seething waters of corruption, the poor waif ultimately drifts to the lee-shore of social and religious hatred. He becomes the restless individual whose sole aim is to pull down and destroy rather than to build up and consolidate. The increase of such a class bodes ill for the future of society. It is to be feared that this unfortunate rabble is increasing by leaps and bounds, and the reason is that even the most eminent non-Catholic educationalists write of the influence of religion in education with almost apologetic pens. They forget that their otherwise admirable school curricula will prove abortive unless a truly religious atmosphere, created by explicit dogma, pervades the school. That atmosphere must blend with, and perfect, the atmosphere of the home. Parental reverence must be complemented by pedagogic reverence. It is only such a concord that can bring about what every educationalist insists upon, i.e., the education of the whole child. It is here that Catholic instinct proves unerring, all the while that educational theorists are beating about for the solution of a difficulty raised by themselves. In all time the Catholic Church has postulated the training of the *whole child*—spiritually, mentally and physically—and has logically insisted on the training going on, in home and in school, during the entire period of childhood. This is synonymous with the atmosphere we have already spoken of.

Modern educationalists also insist on the training of the whole child, but, when confronted with what they call the "religious problem," they first of all limit religious instruction to certain minutes per day, and then sneer at its insufficiency One of the attempted solutions makes, indeed, painful reading. It is to be found in a volume published as recently as 1914 by Edmond Holmes, late Chief Inspector of Schools. In *What Is and What Might Be*, the author advocates the abolition of belief in Original Sin, on the plea that it vitiates education and lowers the child in his own estimation! Having thus got rid of religious dogmatic truth, he and his followers, in their professed wish to educate the whole child, fall back on what deserves only the name of natural religion. How that has failed in France is known to all who are interested in child-life. Mr. Thiselton Mark, BS, Lecturer of Education in the University of Manchester, says, "Under the title *Rationalisme et Tradition*, M. Devolvé has recently published a careful inquiry into the effects of the lay moral instruction in France as compared with the earlier traditional religious instruction. He comes to the conclusion that the dynamic effect of the new teaching upon the moral nature of the scholars is inadequate. And this he believes to be because it fails to attach itself to any living center within the child's nature, around which the elements of the moral life group themselves, as it were, spontaneously, as an organism develops from an original central germ. The traditional religious teaching had such an organic center." *

Educationalists who seek to eliminate the teaching of dogma from the school curriculum really fall short of the standard of efficiency at which they profess to aim. They fail to see that, in excluding from the school a religious atmosphere homogeneous with the child's home, they are striking at the very roots of efficiency. As William Boyd, Lecturer of Education at the University of Glasgow, wisely says, "The proper function of the school at any age, and most of all in early childhood, is to give assistance to the home, in doing the work which, with all its imperfections, it can do better than any other social institution. The mother who allows another to usurp her place in the upbringing of her children does grievous wrong both to the children and to herself." † In the Catholic system the parents place is never usurped. The religious atmosphere of the home is carried into the school only to be intensified—not stifled—by the Catholic teacher.

It is easy to see that this facilitates the teacher's work. Parents and teachers, far from being in opposition, join hands. The children are freed from distractions that would

---

\* *Modern Views on Education,* pp. 249, 250
† *From Locke to Montessori,* p. 262

beset them by the presentment of different views. The impressions made at home are not blunted by those received in school, but rather sharpened. Far from the child being retarded in his secular studies he, on the contrary, makes greater headway, because of the conservation of mental energy. But the cardinal point is this: Caesar receives his due without God being deprived of His rights.

This is our position in demanding a purely Catholic atmosphere for our schools. That demand does not spring from religious antagonism to our non-Catholic brethren. It does not proceed from depreciation of the splendid work done in non-Catholic schools. It is not in opposition to sound theories of education, for, as we have seen, educationalists insist on the training of the whole child. It is simply the outcome of parental reverence for the child—a reverence that seeks a school atmosphere in perfect harmony with the home, and which rightly conceives that one which is either antagonistic, unsympathetic, or indifferent, will spoil the child's career almost in its beginning.

That our position is not better understood is largely due to the fact—as is evident from their writings—that our neighbors regard our holy religion as something conceived in imposture, nurtured in ignorance and superstition, swathed in the bands of formalism, and not only opposed to progress but unable to progress. Such views prove that they fail to grasp even our elementary doctrines. There can be but one answer. Catholics must answer by their deeds. Parents must prove the hollowness of the above assertions by their virtuous, useful lives, and must show the reality of their convictions by fighting every inch of ground that stands between the dogmatism of the secular educationalist, who seeks to fetter them, and the dogmatism which was initiated by Christ, the first Christian Teacher, when He said, "Go and teach all nations ... and behold I am with you all days even to the consummation of the world." * "So then, brethren, we are not the children of the bond-woman, but of the free; by the freedom wherewith Christ has made us free." †

---

\* Mt 28:19, 20
† Gal 4:31

# SEVEN
*Preparation for Marriage*

Our readers may have wondered at our departure from the logical order, which, long before this, would seem to postulate the present chapter. We conceive that the departure is defensible, for it is only by the contemplation of what the home stands for, that the minds of young people can be attuned to proper dispositions. The ruling principle, in education, is to proceed from the known to the unknown. To the young, marriage is an unknown quantity; but the known truths, already set down, throw a flood of light on its dignity and its obligations. The mind is thus all the better prepared for closer study.

Matrimony is a state of life which demands more preliminary thought than is usually given to it. It is the most ancient contract in the world and superior to all others in its object and in its end. For while other contracts have followed in the wake of society, the union of man and woman dates from the time of our first parents. Other contracts have to do with the land and its products; with the fruits of man's ingenuity, or with the works of his hands; this deals with men and women in themselves. The end of all other contracts is circumscribed by the limits of the terrestrial globe: the end of matrimony is, *in a spiritual sense*, lifted to the plane of heaven. On their marriage day husband and wife are reminded of this, inasmuch as they are exhorted to prove worthy of their vocation by walking "hand-in-hand" to heaven.

Now if men and women give deserved attention to all the details and conditions of ordinary contracts, they should deem it reasonable to devote much more attention to the conditions of this, the most important of all. They should not allow it to become the sport of circumstances. They should prepare for, and enter into it, as reasonable beings. It is a contract for life, one on which depends the earthly happiness of the contracting parties and their descendants, to untold generations. It may mean, for one and all, honor or dishonor on the earth, and weal or woe in the next world.

We have already seen how reverence for the child makes for the happiness of the individual, the betterment of the world and the greater glory of God; but before the child brightens the home, nay, before the marriage contract is signed, deep reverence must be conceived for the holy state of matrimony in itself. It should be regarded as a source from which, under God, a life-giving stream flows into the vast river of racial, social and spiritual life that is ever gliding towards the shores of eternity. Future parents should be keenly alive to the necessity of keeping that source pure and undefiled, so that their children may be able to look back on it with pardonable pride, that the race may be able to congratulate itself on this new addition to its resources, and that God may be induced to favor them with all the blessings promised to those who begin this good work in His name.

Those blessings are largely dependent on the knowledge, possessed by marriageable people, of their obligations; for, as we have previously seen, knowledge, in the moral order, is the forerunner of reverence. Only when inspired by reverence can moral duty be done and persevered in to the end. And God's blessings are for the dutiful.

The mere definition of matrimony is enough to suggest deep reflection on the part of all who contemplate that holy and honorable state; and to excite the reverence of all who regard it as a contract which God has so wonderfully sanctioned as to raise it to the dignity of a sacrament, when it is entered into by His Christian children.

Matrimony is the marital union of man and woman in perpetual wedlock, binding them to individual and indissoluble companionship. When we speak of marital union we are to understand that the parties to the contract surrender themselves into each other's keeping; so that, while retaining their freedom of will they, nevertheless, use that freedom for the recognition of each other's rights. Matrimonially speaking, the right of the husband is to be the head of the wife—the right and the privilege of the wife is to obey. No woman who loves a man in a righteous way will regard it other than a privilege to obey, when he as her lawfully wedded husband, leads her forth from the church. Should any woman dispute the right, or contemn the privilege, let her prove her conviction by abstaining from the contract; for obedience is one of its essential conditions. The wife belongs to the husband and the husband to the wife, subject to the conditions laid down by our Holy Mother the Church, to whom Almighty God has committed the care of the Seven Sacraments instituted by Himself. This means that they are one and are to remain as one, as long as the life of either lasts, as is evident from the remaining part of the definition. Needless to say, the definition itself is based on very clear scriptural texts: "A man shall leave his father and mother, and shall cleave to his wife. And they two shall be in one flesh. Therefore now they are not two but one flesh. What, therefore, God has joined together, let no man put asunder." \* "But to them that are married, not I but the Lord commands that the wife depart not from her husband ... And let not the husband put away his wife." †

The simple statement of these truths shows the rashness of rushing into matrimony before the attainment of an age when the parties to the contract can reason maturely on all that is involved by them. They run the risk of "marrying in haste and repenting at leisure." The truths above set down point to the wisdom of young people lending a more willing ear than is customary to the suggestions of their parents, and of others capable of advising them, with regard to the qualities that should be found in a life partner; and also with regard to the conditions of the contract they propose to enter upon. Furthermore, they demand a much more confidential and sympathetic attitude on the part of parents towards those children who are approaching manhood and womanhood, for many of the evils that are current are due to reticence on this fundamental question.

---

\* Mk 10:7-9
† I Cor 7:10-11

If young people are left altogether to themselves, or if they arrogate to themselves a sufficiency of judgement, they become inflated with the idea that their mutual love will enable them to surmount all the difficulties that may present themselves. This confidence on the part of the young is not a thing to be despised. If the love be pure and elevated, it is rather to be admired. But they should be gently led to see that it is not enough. It has not sufficient depth. For love to have depth and stability, it must be founded on knowledge. In immature youth, it is too much to expect that knowledge of the qualities necessary in a life-long partner will be sufficiently precise. Young people are easily smitten by external qualities that will have little or no bearing on future cravings of the heart; hence the necessity of keeping their hearts free until their heads are so sufficiently stocked with knowledge as to lead them aright. For if mutual love be not interwoven with sturdy common sense, and with a clear understanding of what matrimony means, it will not stand the strain to which, in later years, it will be subjected.

The old proverb has it that "when poverty enters the door, love flies out of the window." It is capable of a much wider application than the obvious one, and, in the wider application, it is more frequently verified. Material poverty has been known to deepen and intensify mutual love. Lovers who were drifting apart from each other in a mansion have been known to discover true love only when poverty drove them into a cottage. It is, rather, mental and spiritual poverty which, when it enters in, or is—far too late—discovered, drives love away. What a terrible crisis, in married life, to wake up to the fact that while one had beauty, and polish, and education, she had no heart! Or that while the other had money, and ability, and social influence, he had no domestic virtues!

Now it is precisely here that mature judgement is necessary. The love of young people is, more likely than not, to base itself on graces of body or manner. Good looks and winsome ways on the part of a young woman are quite sufficient to turn the head of the average young man. A certain dash and enthusiasm on the part of a young man— nay, sometimes, a positive leaning to recklessness—are enough to make him appear a hero to the ordinary young woman. If, on the strength of these unstable foundations, a home be set up, who does not see that a very slight domestic storm will be sufficient to raze it to the ground? May not this be the cause of many of the unholy separations witnessed at the present day? Human respect, as a rule, saves those in the higher grades of *Catholic* society; but in the humbler walks of life we, too often, find that before the first anniversary of a marriage can be held, husband and wife are disillusioned and disappointed. Intoxicated with what they thought was love, they discovered, to their dismay, that it was but passion or sentimentality.

The inference is that such marriages were entered into without mature judgement, that superficial qualities were, alone, considered, and that the contracting parties were substantially ignorant of what marriage really meant. Now, a certain degree of sentimentality must, perforce, enter into a contract which appeals so intimately to the emotions, but when that degree has been exaggerated so as to blind the parties to well-defined incompatibility of temperament they expose themselves to untold misery in after-life. While a true Christian marriage, when the partners are well mated, is a source of mutual consolation and strength; on the other hand it involves mutual forbearance, tact, self-sacrifice, patience, obedience, trust, drudgery, humiliations, weariness and monotony; and those only who face it with at least some knowledge of this long catalog of probabilities, but who, nevertheless, mean to persevere, hand-in-hand to the end, can be said to love each other in God.

If it be asked, "Where has love a place in such a catalog?" the answer is that it is love alone can make all those limitations bearable. Short of true, self-sacrificing love, marriage could not long endure. When the love is superficial, and based only on externals, it lasts only so long as those externals are found intact. For love to endure it must have rested on a more substantial foundation. The sacredness of matrimony must have been understood and its conditions must have been grasped. Love should mean the inviolable observance of those conditions to the end of life.

Now the only rational form of love between man and woman is that which is in keeping with the law of God: "If any man love Me, let him keep My commandments." Young people, contemplating matrimony, should ring the changes on these words, saying, "If we love each other, let us prove our love by, first of all, loving God, through the keeping of His commandments. For vain will be all our protestations of love for each other if, under cover of them, we offend God. To be true to God, we must first, to ourselves, be true."

That this true and exalted love may be deepened, the young folks must remember that the contract they contemplate entering into is also a sacrament. The mere fact of the contracting parties being baptized makes it such. The Church declares that the contract of matrimony between baptized persons is inseparable from the sacrament. During the period of the engagement prior to marriage this important fact should loom up before their minds at once as a guiding star and a danger signal—a star to lead them to the practice of virtue, a signal to ward off danger. In their hearts they should feel that the efficacy of the sacrament will depend much on their worthiness, and they should determine to approach it with such innocence of soul and purity of body as will merit for them the grace of the sacrament and the blessing of the Church.

The fact that matrimony is such a sacred institution and that it has such far-reaching consequences will, naturally, lead thoughtful young people to inquire into the conditions necessary for its validity, its lawfulness and its use. It is here that there is much room for improvement in the manner of helping those who are called by God to this holy vocation. Too often, through mistaken notions of modesty, this holy contract is the one least explained, and, as a consequence, the one most exposed to the wiles of the ungodly. Impediments, rules and regulations are, so to speak, flung at young people as if they were missiles intended to hurt, all the while that they are ordinances of the Church meant to save. Fathers of families are mute, mothers are mysterious, and so, when information is obtained, it is often by stealthy methods, in questionable quarters, and of a doubtful kind.

Parents should understand that, when their children are of marriageable age, they have every right to know the meaning of that particular form of life, and that, if they ask, they have a perfect right to be informed of the nature of its obligations. And when the reception of the sacrament is imminent, no parent, worthy of the name, should rest content unless quite assured that the young aspirant understands all that is involved by the contract. It requires but a very few well-chosen words, and, if parents feel a native delicacy in being communicative, they should suggest a quiet talk with some decent Catholic friend. Lifelong misery has often resulted from the—let me call it—unnatural silence of those whose office it is to help to avert disaster. In no other contract under the sun does this strange conduct hold. How pitiful that it should exist in connection with the most venerable and the most important contract in the world! No wonder that some of our young people make mistakes; the wonder is that they are not more numerous. No wonder that scandals exist! Such mistakes and scandals are due less to the bad intentions of the young folks than to the incompetence of their elders.

Let it be understood that, as I am dealing solely with home life, I am not voicing an opinion as to the expediency or non-expediency of instructing school-children; although, as a matter of fact, I am opposed to such teaching. I am rigidly confining my view to young people of marriageable age. When, at that age, mild curiosity is awakened, with regard to what is most vital in society, it is simply unpardonable to attempt to burke inquiry. If the veil of so-called mystery be not raised with reverent hands by those whose office it is to guide; if pertinent questions be not candidly answered; if it be suggested that the matter is taboo amongst God-fearing people, then the bewildered youths will be, perforce, thrown upon the tender mercies of hundreds round about, who treat this fundamental question with anything but a reverent spirit. To this, again, must be ascribed many of the evils that abound. It is useless to declaim against the evils of race suicide, the scandals of divorce, the villainies of seduction, all the while that young people are left to their own surmises, on the plea that "where ignorance is bliss, 'tis folly to be wise." Ignorance with regard to the conditions of a contract is not bliss—it is stupidity. Ignorance with regard to this, the most important of all contracts, is not bliss, nor is it true modesty—it is criminal, because it is founded on injustice. For it is an injustice to young people to allow them to bind themselves for life in ignorance of the major details of their duties. It is to leave them to gambol in the moonshine of sentimentality, all the while that their future will bristle with hard facts.

The root of the evil of over-reticence springs really from the soil of irreverence. There can be no real reverence entertained for young people if it be too readily supposed that they are curious with wrong intent. The more charitable and the more just view is that their curiosity is entirely wholesome. It should be supposed that they wish to know, simply that they may act rightly. One who wishes to do wrong asks no questions. He is a law to himself. His mind is already made up. And in putting questions, our young people are not prying into mysteries. There can be no mystery about a human contract. If they are informed in a sympathetic, straightforward and reverent manner, they will be led to bless and to praise the great Creator, they will prove zealous supporters of the Church in her wise legislation, their reverence for the state of Matrimony will be deepened, and they will be saved from the clutches of those whose conversation is lewd, and from the bad impressions made by books that are vile.

Too much reticence is an irreverence to God and His works and His sanctions. It is made appear that some of

His ordinances are almost uncanny, all the while that they are the fruits of His wisdom and His power.

The problem for the person of whom information is asked is to know whether the motive of the inquirer is good or bad. If the person be of a suitable age, the only motive that can be imputed as evil is that of pruriency, i.e., a desire for knowledge merely for the gratification of morbid curiosity.

When, from the lips of the truly reverent, adequate information reaches the minds of sensible young people, the way is paved for the easy understanding of the legislation of the Church. The laws of the Church seem hard and fast only to the ignorant. Once our young people grasp the real dignity of matrimony, as the divinely appointed means to people the earth with children legitimately born, healthy in body and holy in soul, honorable in their progenitors and with hopes of a happy immortality, it is marvelous how easily they grasp the reasonableness of the laws regarding consanguinity, affinity, spiritual relationship, and the others that are promulgated as safeguards of this great sacrament. Full knowledge, reverently imparted, informs them of the part they have to play in co-operating with the creative work of God, and is more likely to save them from mutual dangers than a thousand head-shakings and a million muffled sentences.

In fine, if parents strive to be more companionable with their grown-up children, and if mothers especially take their daughters to their hearts and give them their confidence, they may rest assured that confidences will be given in return. Trained thus, the young women will become the earthly angel-guardians of the young men, whose company they keep with a view to matrimony, and the result will be an approach to the altar in a befitting manner. For a considerable time marriage has loomed up before them as the greatest of all contracts; their knowledge of its obligations has inspired mutual respect; they have loved to receive Holy Communion regularly, by way of preparation; they have thus disposed themselves for the Nuptial Blessing, and, as long as life lasts, they will look back on the chaste days of courtship with gladness of heart for that chastity was the outcome, under God, of the deep reverence they entertained for the holy state which it is now their privilege to enjoy.

# EIGHT
## Mixed Marriages

THE legislation of the Church with regard to mixed marriages does not meet with the sympathy it deserves. Outside the Fold it is treated with ill-concealed contempt, and, within, it is—in some quarters—far from being welcomed with a docile spirit. Let us hope that this lack of docility proceeds more from misunderstanding than from want of good will; for if the latter could, in all cases, be alleged, we should have reason to fear for the future of the Church and for the peace and happiness of the home. As mixed marriages seem, in divers places, to be on the increase, it would bode ill for Catholicity if it could be proved that they are the result of stubbornness on the side of the Catholic partner. It seems to us that although self-will and, in some rare cases, a positively bad will, do precipitate such marriages, the great majority of them are due to failure in grasping the importance of the principles that are at stake. We are convinced that if the young folk, who now murmur and complain about the strictness of matrimonial legislation, had patience enough to consider the matter in all its bearings, they would become more amenable to the laws of the Church.

As a preliminary to right understanding, our readers are asked to accept it as an historic fact that the Church, from its institution, has been, and now is, a true and tender mother; for, unless this fact be accepted and kept in mind, the legislation of the Church will tend to irritate rather than to conciliate. It seems to us that forgetfulness of this very point is chiefly responsible for the modern spirit of irreverence and disobedience. The primary instinct of a true mother is the safety of her children. She toils, she suffers, she makes untold sacrifices for the sake of her offspring. She is content to sow in tears so long as she can reasonably hope that her children will reap in joy. When she points out a line of duty, it is because her insight and her experience assure her that it is the safest one for them to follow. When she inflicts pains and penalties, it is because she loves those whom she has brought into the world: "He who spares the rod hates the child." * This, which is perfectly true of our mothers according to the flesh—provided they rise to the level of their responsibilities—is especially true of our spiritual mother, the Church; but with this important distinction that the Church is incomparably more enlightened, even in her disciplinary legislation, than the ordinary members of the Fold. Now it is surely not expecting too much from our young people, who have been baptized into, and brought up in, the One True Church, to make themselves acquainted with her mind in the important matter under discussion. For the Church cannot have existed through so many ages without having

---

* Pv 13:24

made up her mind, in one way or the other. Moreover, being the Spouse of Christ, illumined and assisted by the Holy Ghost, and divinely appointed to be our teacher and our unerring guide, she could not possibly have made up her mind in a manner at variance with the best interests of her children: "Can a mother forget her child?"

It is here, however, that some of our young folks profess to be rather perplexed. On the one hand, they are told that the Church has always been, and that it still is, strongly opposed to mixed marriages, while on the other, they are well aware that dispensations for the celebration of such are granted in all parts of the world. When they reflect that large numbers of mixed marriages are contracted in Great Britain, they are led to assume, far too readily, that the legislation of the Church need not be taken seriously and that, as dispensations have been conceded to others, they will, as a matter of course, be granted to themselves. If externals only were in question, the above reasoning would be justifiable, for the frequency of mixed marriages in Britain has become notorious; but our readers must remember that every single marriage of that kind has been prefaced by the sifting of evidence, and that the Church has dispensed solely on the ground that the evidence was sufficient to justify its action. But, even in the act of dispensing, she shows her displeasure by withholding her blessing.

She discountenances them because of her long and intimate knowledge of their dangers; but in cases where she fears that, by not dispensing, *graver* dangers may be induced, she relaxes her law. It must not be inferred that this is the doing of evil that good may come: it is rather choosing the lesser of two evils. The Church considers it an evil that the holy state of matrimony should be entered into by those whose minds are divided on the subject of Faith, but that the evil would be greater if the misguided partners elected to live in sin. In granting a dispensation she exacts promises which, if kept, will be likely to safeguard the Faith of the Catholic partner and all the children of the marriage; and if the conditions laid down by her seem hard, it must be remembered that every word thereof is suggested by the holy Spirit of God who is her guide. "He that hears you hears Me." *

If, in a spirit of holiness, wisdom and justice, the Church has been led to legislate, as above, she has also been led to relax her laws according to the needs of time and place. In the beginnings of Christian society, when the pagans enormously exceeded the Christians in number, it is evident that if she had not relaxed the law, by granting dispensations for the marriage of believers with unbelievers, the growth of Christianity would have been retarded. In those early days the Christians were so strong in the Faith and so fervent in the practice of their holy religion that she had every hope of a large harvest of souls through the concessions she granted. At that time, so great was her solicitude for the spiritual welfare of her children, that if two unbelievers had contracted matrimony, and one of them became a convert to the Faith, the latter had the right to repudiate the other, if he or she refused to allow the convert the peaceable exercise of the true religion. To this day, this privilege—promulgated by St. Paul, and therefore called "The Pauline Privilege"—is in force in pagan countries. It may be here remarked that the Church bars mar-

---

* Lk 10:16

riage with an *unbaptized* person by what is called a diriment impediment, i.e., an impediment which renders such a marriage null and void, short of a dispensation having been asked and obtained. As the world grew older and heresies arose which occasioned their adherents being cut off from the One True Church, a state of things arose somewhat similar to that which existed in earlier days. In districts almost depopulated of Catholics by bloody persecution it was, humanly speaking, necessary to dispense, and thus we find dispensations granted for the celebration of what is called a mixed marriage, i.e., the marriage of a Catholic with one who has been baptized in some church other than the true one. The impediment to a marriage of this kind, although prohibitive, did not render the marriage null and void, but, if contracted without a dispensation, it put the Catholic party under the ban of mortal sin and deprived the marriage of the blessing of the Church. Even in granting dispensations, the Church reprobated such unions, unless the circumstances were of such a nature as to render them absolutely necessary, as the lesser of two evils.

According to a general law of the Church, it may be broadly said that, since Easter, 1908, any marriage between two Catholics, or between a Catholic and a baptized non-Catholic, which has not been celebrated before a duly approved Catholic priest and two witnesses is invalid, and this invalidity will apply to all such marriages in the future.

Now that we have tried to disclose the mind of the Church with regard to mixed marriages, we should ask our young men whether they can conscientiously say that the conditions of modern life are of such a nature as to necessitate the relaxation of the law on their behalf. Can they say with truth that, in Great Britain, there is such a dearth of eligible Catholic partners as warrants their seeking the life long companionship of those who are outside the Fold? If, in one particular locality, there be a dearth of desirable Catholic families, are not the means of communication with more favored districts sufficiently easy to admit of their going farther afield in search of wives who will bring God's blessing on them and their future homes? If a young man think nothing at all of scouring the country in search of better conditions of labor, is it too much to ask him to take at least *some* pains in seeking a life partner of his own Faith?

Short of making serious efforts to seek and find a Catholic wife, it would be most unfair on the part of a marriageable young man to say, "The Church has dispensed others—why should not I enjoy a like privilege?" Our tender Mother, the Church, much as she reprobates it, will also dispense him, if sufficient reasons be given, but the onus (and it is a serious one) lies on him of, first of all, taking at least *some* pains to win the love of one who is a faithful member of the Church.

Seeing that, in populous districts, there are hundreds of splendid Catholic young women to choose from, it is evident that our Catholic young men who contract mixed marriages have not put themselves to any particular trouble in endeavoring to secure that most precious of all earthly treasures, a good Catholic wife. It is an insult to those excellent young women, nay it is an insult offered to our Holy Mother the Church, and is well calculated to bring upon her the sneers and scoffs of Protestant critics, who find her bringing up young women with the most tender solicitude, only to have them despised and rejected by the young men of their Faith.

From the spirit in which these chapters are written, our readers will, it is to be hoped, agree that we have nothing whatsoever to say against our non-Catholic friends, as neighbors and fellow-workers. But in the pursuit of our project of setting forth the principles that are conducive to the holiness and happiness of the home we should not be true to those principles if we did not try to make it clear that religion is the very corner-stone of true happiness. From the moment that the young couple kneel at the altar for the Nuptial Blessing until the time comes when one or other will be carried to the grave it is religion that will be found their most durable support and their deepest consolation. The strength of the husband will decay and the beauty of the wife will fade; many will be the vicissitudes of their lives—sunshine and storm, success and failure, health and sickness—but if there be unity in the Faith, and in the exercise of their religious duties, balm will be found for every wound, resignation will lighten every cross, and perseverance to the end, in supernatural love, will be assured.

Would to God that every young man of marriageable age faced his future fairly and squarely, and reasoned with himself somewhat after the following fashion: Now that I mean to set up a home, what woman is the more likely to prove all that a wife should be? I am a Catholic—a descendant of those who suffered for the Faith once delivered by Jesus Christ. My Faith has been purchased at a great price. It has been handed down to me at the cost of many sacrifices. Loyalty and gratitude should fill me with a great desire to pass it on to future generations. It can only be perpetuated — so far as I am concerned — by the choice of a partner who believes in the One True Church. My marriage can be blessed and sanctified only through a union with one who believes it to form one of the Seven Sacraments. My peace can be secured only through a union with one who accepts all the teaching of the Church. Short of that, there would be endless confusion: a clashing of interests, and the intervention of outsiders in my most sacred family affairs. Each baptism would mean a quarrel; each send-off of children to school would mean a bitter discussion; every Sunday would bring with it divergence of view in the thing that really matters — religion. If my wife be a non-Catholic, she cannot possibly infuse into the minds and hearts of my children what she has not received, namely, a tender love of Mary my Mother, respect for the Church, reverence for the priesthood. My own mother had easier access to my heart than my father. So will it be with my children. When I am absent, toiling for bread, my wife, their mother, will be engaged in forming their characters. She may, from many points of view, be altogether excellent, but how can she be expected to form the characters of my children as I could wish? No matter how fair she may be, no matter how thrifty, no matter how loyal and true, a time will come when most of the sweetness of life will be derived from the consolations of religion, but in that we shall be as apart as the poles. In the name of God, how *could* I face such a sea of dangers without fearing shipwreck?

We feel that if all our fine young men reasoned on these lines, prayed over the matter, and took counsel with their parents and priests, the Church would be preserved from many of the anxieties and scandals that now oppress her, and homes would be happier by far.

As compared with our young men, our young women are hampered by the limitations of their sex, for they are debarred from proposing marriage. But, although thus handicapped, they have it in their power to prove their loyalty and their spirit by refusing all offers of marriage that come from outside sources. It may demand sacrifices almost equivalent to that of martyrdom, but God will bless them with an adequate reward even in the present life. We are convinced that if our Catholic young women showed more independence of spirit and absolutely refused all advances until the applicant consented to be introduced to a priest, for enlightenment on our doctrines, there would be fewer broken hearts and spoiled lives in matrimonial circles. In too many cases our young women allow their hearts to be stolen away without a single interchange of views about the only thing that really matters in life—religion. Courtships sometimes endure for years without any attempt being made to bring the non-Catholic suitor any nearer to the Church.

Now we hold it to be the bounden duty of every Catholic young woman who loves her Faith, and who values her reputation, to make it perfectly clear to the person who seeks her hand that she is a Catholic and that her religion must ever have the first claim on her affections. She may take it for granted that a good honorable young man, far from being displeased, will be very much impressed. He will feel that he is dealing with an equally honorable person, and will not refuse to inquire into the tenets of a religion that has infused such spirit into the girl who has attracted him.

As it would be an endless task to discuss all the possibilities that confront young women in these busy days, when they are plunged so deeply into the non-Catholic business world, let us content ourselves with suggesting some few points for reflection on the lines followed when addressing our young men.

From what we have said regarding a mother's influence in the formation of the character of her children our young women might imagine that even although the father be a non-Catholic all will be well, provided that they themselves be true to the Faith. This reasoning might be sound enough if they had their husbands only to reckon with; but experience proves that non-Catholic husbands, even after ready compliance with the conditions laid down by the Church, become strangely susceptible to the subtle influence exercised by their relatives. In many cases that baneful influence endures as long as life lasts, and the Catholic wife and mother finds herself a mere domestic in her own home, doomed to minister but to the bodily wants of husband and children, all the while that the higher aspirations of her soul are bound in chains. Children baptized almost by stealth in the Catholic Church grow up but to have their faith undermined in Protestant schools, and, through habitual intercourse with Protestant relatives and friends, find themselves almost foreordained to perpetuate the mistake made first by their own unhappy mother by marrying outside the Church. The priest is often denied admission to the home; obstacles are put in the way of hearing Mass on Sundays; the gross tales current in Protestant circles about the confessional lead to confession being banned, and cases are on record that, even in her last hours, the poor victim has been willfully deprived of the last consolations of her holy Faith. These statements, which, when put into cold print, seem so unnatural and so horrible, can be vouched for by every priest of experience. Even were they verified in only one case out of a hundred, what woman would wish them to be verified in her own life? And what guarantee can she have that they may not be verified, if she runs the risk? Even when a mixed marriage seems, to the outside world, to run on smooth lines, if we got a candid avowal from the parties to that marriage they would unite in saying: "Well, yes! things go smoothly enough; but, after all, there is a want!" The thing that is wanting, and that no human comfort or pleasure can supply, is *unity in the Faith*.

Apart from the foregoing considerations there are others that should weigh with intelligent, God-fearing, wholesome-minded young women. We need but mention the unnatural views held by so many non-Catholics regarding limitation of the family and the erroneous opinions entertained regarding divorce.

Although the scope of this work does not admit of our entering into all the details of this subject, we trust that enough has been said to lead our young people to treat it with a seriousness befitting its importance, to pray with all their hearts that God may direct them for the best, and to put their confidence in some kind and prudent [spiritual] director when there is question of their settlement in life. To all young people of marriageable age we heartily recommend the very complete volume on Holy Matrimony published by Fr. de Zulueta, SJ.*

---

\* *Letters on Christian Doctrine*, vol. 3

# NINE
*Husband and Wife*

COURTSHIP, no matter how prolonged, does not draw aside the veil that hides the future. Lovers become husband and wife without *really* understanding each other. Although "the course of true love never yet ran smooth," the occasional ripples seldom or never disturb the waters down to their very depths. And so, man and woman may become husband and wife without gauging each other's power to make wedded life happy or miserable. Even when both are equipped with sufficient knowledge of the duties of their future state, and have brought that knowledge to bear on their mutual choice, the contemplated change of life is surrounded with mystery. The laws of health may be perfectly understood, and by those laws the parties may have been influenced in giving hand and word; the relatives on either side may have been studied and approved of; ways and means of living may have been discussed; the future may have projected itself on the screen as a dream of bliss, but time alone can tell whether that dream will come true.

It is well that it is so. This mysteriousness lends a peculiar charm to the undertaking. Where every winding of a road is known, and when pilgrims are able to locate each knoll and milestone, the journey is robbed of much of its enchantment. Courtship, reverently and innocently indulged in, reveals the broad lines of temperament and enables the lovers to see whether they are suited for each other, but it leaves thousands of details unnoticed. For love is blind. Where appreciation enters in, it is always so. In art, providing the scheme of color satisfies and the composition of the picture is good, the work holds us spellbound for many a day. As time goes on, minor details that run counter to the canons of art may be discerned, but they fail to undermine our appreciation. Had we, to begin with, fastened on those slight failings, we should have been robbed of our joy. It is sometimes good to be blind. The physically blind are proverbial for the radiance of their countenance. Those who are blind to the little failings of their neighbors are remarkable for the warmth of their hearts. Love is blind.

Thus it is that wedded life begins with a great fund of faith and trust. Husband and wife leave their old homes with high hopes of building even a better one; faith in their power to do so is very strong; and God, in His love and mercy enriches them with sacramental grace to enable them to love each other more and more, to bear the burdens He may lay upon them, and to bring up their children in His fear and love. Thus gifted, their fund of faith and trust should never run short: their happiness need never become bankrupt. But, as someone has said, "the measure of happiness in marriage is usually in proportion to one's deserts." If husband and wife would have full measure, they must work for it. To *get* they must *give*. Happiness does not come, as if by magic, when the ring is put on the finger and when mutual troth is plighted. It is the reward of sacrifices on both sides. If, on either side, there be selfishness, love is crushed. Duty may still be done by the wounded party, and merit will be gained in the sight of Heaven; but Heaven would be better pleased and the earth made more joyous if *both* parties merited by mutual sacrifices.

The mysterious future of husband and wife is heavily laden with possibilities. The health of either may break down; relatives may prove unsympathetic or unfriendly; husband or wife may betray instability with regard to faith or morals; some hereditary taint may reveal itself; the social success or failure of a husband may occasion a cleavage—in a word, a thousand and one things may intervene to interrupt the dream of bliss that they promised themselves. It is in such junctures that their Faith must come to the rescue. They must keep steadily and constantly in remembrance that they are ministers of a great sacrament, whose graces will not be denied them if they do their humble best to keep their pact. They must keep the sacred fire of love burning within them, by recalling to mind the excellencies they saw in each other in bygone days. They must pray for each other. They must hope against hope for better things and in their individual conduct guard against being a rock of offense to each other.

Addressing myself first to the husband, I should ask him to show the true manliness of his character by his chivalry, his strength, his generosity and his tenderness. In the days of courtship he was all that. But for the exhibition of those qualities he could not possibly have won his wife.

They stole her heart away. What a catastrophe if she now discovers that they were but phantoms of her own mind and that there is no reality behind! Although now a wife, she is still a woman—the weaker vessel—and, therefore, worships chivalry, loves to lean on a strong arm, hungers for generosity, and is prepared to melt away when treated tenderly. And she has now a greater right than of yore to claim all that her husband can give, for she has surrendered herself into his keeping. In his service the color has faded from her cheeks, lines of care have been traced on her brow, threads of silver have become interwoven with her hair, new and strange maladies have invaded her constitution. She is conscious of it all, and, as the consciousness deepens, oh, how her heart yearns for the retention of the love that once was so generously given. Child-bearing, house keeping, nursing, watching, saving, have pressed most heavily on her, all the while that he is scatheless. What a shame it would be for our common manhood if, while the wife bears all those traces of self-sacrifice, the husband made use of his immunity to live a free and easy life, and so add one more pang to the many that she has suffered for his sake—the pang of jealousy.

God forbid it should be so, but there is reason to fear that it may be so, unless husbands ponder deeply over what wifehood and motherhood mean to a woman. It seems to me that there is ample room for improvement. Many husbands forswear out-of-door companionship with their wives after the birth of the first child; others are so immersed in business as to seem to regret, as time lost, the hours they must, perforce, spend at home; few think of making spontaneous presents, or of providing some little delicacy in times of sickness or depression. They take all and give nothing. They are thoughtless, tactless, brusque, impolite and unsympathetic. They never pause to reflect on the monotony of home life, its drudgery, its burdens, its needs, its humiliations, otherwise they would surely strive to be more companionable, helpful, open-handed, loving and tender. They should remember that a woman's craving for love does not die when the wedding-ring is put on. In that hour she obtains a sanction from Heaven to love more and more, and she regards her life, from a human point of view, as a failure, unless her love is requited. True, her every child enables her to be lavish of it and to obtain it, but she craves for proofs of it, to the end, from her husband. He must give proofs by being God-fearing, sober, hard-working, chivalrous, strong in character yet kind and tender. What is this but saying that he should continue to be all that he gave promise of when she consented to kneel by his side at the altar?

The wife must contribute to the happiness of the home by keeping alive the admiration that she evinced for her husband in the happy days of courtship. He was then her hero. If he shows a tendency to wander from the line of rectitude, let it be her holy ambition to lead him back. If the love of a faithful wife and a tender mother prove ineffective, he must have wandered very far indeed. But it is to be feared that, in many instances, the wanderings of the husband can be traced to the lack of good judgement on the part of the wife. The wife must remember that the husband is head of the house and that, as such, he is to be respected, loved, obeyed and supported. He looked for this when he chose her out of a thousand. Granted that the young couple brought the grace of God on their courtship by leading good lives, that they exercised their reason in making a choice, and that they sought the advice of their parents on their momentous undertaking, it cannot be supposed that either husband or wife will stray very far without some preliminary stages. Now it is precisely here that a wife needs all the judgement at her command. Her solicitude for her husband's soul must never lead her to assume the role of a judge. She must beware of nagging. She must guard against posing as a neglected wife. And it is fatal to betray jealousy.

The exercise of good judgement should point the way to sacrifice. Sacrifice means self-repression. Let it be granted that the husband has faults—glaring faults. From what has been already said, it must be evident that the writer is not blind to them. The wife is not asked to condone them, but she is expected to do her best to dissipate them. Let her, first of all, repress the bitter reproach that rises to her lips; the desire to confront him with his accumulated offenses; the threat to treat him as she herself has been treated. In one word, let her be patient: "Patience has a perfect work." * Possessing her soul in patience, she will find herself confronted with some very pertinent questions. Conscience will ask: Have you respected your husband (and yourself) by your attention to dress, cleanliness, order, punctuality, thrift and respectability? Have you shown your love by your interest in all that concerns his welfare—his family, his business, his tasks, his ambitions? Have you obeyed him in all matters that pertain to the matrimonial life, and that are in keeping with the law of God? Have you supported him in his trials, soothed him in his sorrows, helped him in his anxieties, encouraged him in his enter-

---

* Jms 1:4

prises, and cheered him on to do even better things for God, society, and his family? If conscience is not satisfied with the replies, the wife should not rest until satisfaction comes. When the day happily dawns in which a wife can conscientiously say that she is satisfied with her efforts on behalf of her husband, she will probably find that he has become all that she wished him to be. He was, all the while, waiting for practical proofs of her love. Some writer has said that, in the main, the world's best work has been done by the married, through the powerful influence exercised by true affection.

If this be true, the wife who is faithful to her mission can claim the lion's share, for she is, to a large extent, the keeper of her husband's soul. Her position in the household, as wife and mother, is a reflex of the loving Providence that watches over humanity. She has in her keeping the bread-winner and the little ones for whom bread is won. If her love be tender and true, the household will be as wax in her hands. The husband will feel all the stronger and mightier because of her unassuming influence, and the children will forever be proud of the parents who handed down to them the family name, and, with that name, an undying spirit of rectitude.

Truly, "a virtuous wife is a crown to her husband," and "the heart of her husband does safely trust in her."[*] And a virtuous husband looms up before a wife as her earthly idol. His noble, manly brow catches the light that beams from heaven; his arms, so strong in toil, are, to her, as soft and tender as those of the baby who nestles on her bosom; his voice, so imperative without, is mild and persuasive

---

[*] Pv 12:4; 31:11

within his home. She delights in acknowledging that he is lord and master, for never once does he abuse his power. The silver jubilee—nay, the golden jubilee—of the marriage-day may be celebrated, but the backward glance over years checkered with hopes and fears, successes and failures, health and sickness, joys and sorrows, discovers no real cleavage in their interests. In those bygone years God made them one. They have never ceased to be one: one in body and one in soul—worshipping as one, suffering as one, rejoicing as one, hoping as one, and longing so to die, in the grace of God, as to be one with Him for ever in heaven.

This happiness of husband and wife is the fruit of correspondence with the precious graces bestowed in the Sacrament of Matrimony. Although that sacrament involved complete mutual surrender and inviolable companionship, neither the surrender nor the close companionship occasioned the slightest loss of personal dignity. The flight of years found the husband improving in the arts of politeness, considerateness, tenderness and sympathy that made him so commendable when he was paying his suit as a lover. In those days he *surmised* that the girl he loved was all that his heart could hope for, to make it glad. The passing years have *convinced* him that he was right. His ever-growing courtesy is, to him, but an act of gratitude for all that God has bestowed. The happiness of the wife is largely due to the fact that she has never ceased to recognize the value of the prize she was won. Her daily prayer and her every Communion have been availed of to thank the Giver of every good gift. Her womanly instinct has continually suggested new ways and means of honoring and of pleasing her heart's adored one. After God, her husband has been her all. No wonder then that, although she has aged, she still retains her youthful charm. No wonder that she has retained his affection to the last. It is the deep consciousness of that possession that completes her happiness. It was for that she left the old home. Even when she is wrapt in the vision of God, she hopes to retain it in the new home.

# TEN
*Parentage*

EVERY succeeding age draws aside, little by little, the veil of prejudice and reveals to men of good will the wisdom of Church legislation. In our own day this has been strikingly evinced with regard to the indissolubility of consummated matrimony, the importance of religion in the education of the child, the need of an Index of prohibited books, and the problem of race-suicide. No matter what his creed, every self-respecting thinker admires the attitude of the Church regarding marriage; educationalists cannot but see the logic of the Catholic position in school affairs; moralists are, themselves, pleading for the censorship of published matter; and the saner portion of the medical faculty, legislators and philanthropists, point to the Catholic Church as the one great institution which takes a firm and intelligent stand against that abuse of matrimony which is known to all newspaper readers as race-suicide.

Looking to the publicity acquired by this modern evil, it would be mere affectation to apologize for its introduction to these pages. When the sluices of Satan's reservoirs are widely opened and we find our young people in danger of being swept off their feet by the devastating flood, we need not apologize for stretching out a helping hand. That flood has been rushing madly on for many years. It has inundated France and made it almost a barren waste. It is gradually submerging England. It threatens the whole civilized world. Statesmen look on it with dismay, for it is calculated to undermine the foundations of Empire; medical men behold in it not only the loss of beings that might have existed, but the mental and physical enfeeblement of those who are responsible for the dearth; legislators are in a state of panic and are preparing schemes for the coaxing or coercing of married people to be not only married, but prolific.

From this gloomy background, how splendidly the Church stands out! In all the centuries of her existence, her attitude has been that of the upholder of the natural law, the defender of the home, the protector of the child. With her it is not primarily a question of Empire, or prosperity, or health: it is simply a question of rectitude. But she has always known and has always taught that if the line of rectitude be adhered to, and followed to its logical end, all will be well with a country—morally, intellectually and physically. Brute strength, from without, may assail such a country and, for a time prevail, but, as it is sound within, it will ultimately recover.

True to her commission to teach, the Church has ever proclaimed the dignity of parentage, all the while that she has exalted the vocation to celibacy. She has never exalted the vocation to celibacy at the expense or to the detriment of matrimony. She blesses both.

Her policy makes us aware that the remedy for existing evils is not to be found in the briberies of governments, or in the theories of Eugenists; it is to be found only in a deep reverence for parentage. There would be no need at all for the sickening craving for legislation that now prevails, neither would the privacy of the poor man's home be threatened with invasion by theoretical busybodies, if the world but waked up to the wisdom of listening to the teaching Church, and became alive to the necessity of reducing her maxims to practice.

But even should the outside world **elect** to stand aloof in cold admiration of the logic of the **Church**, it is surely not asking too much to request Her **children** to listen to Her voice and to keep their feet firmly **planted** on the safe shore of the natural law. Fast and **furious, p**olluted and destroying, may be the tide rushing **on, but they** and their offspring will be saved; and when **periodical enumeration** of the peoples be made, it will be **found that** the Church of God is coming into its own. It will be a question of the survival of the fittest—and the fittest are they who hold fast by the law of nature. They who refuse its burdens go to the wall.

Some may have smiled at the suggestion made in our last chapter regarding the pains a young man should take to secure a good Catholic wife. The aptness of the suggestion will be admitted by all who grasp what is meant by parentage. Looked at superficially, as the exercise of functions by which the world is peopled, parentage seems very ordinary and barely rises above the level of what is happening, all around, in animal life; but believers in the immortality of the human soul look at it in a different light, and find it raised to an indescribably higher plane.

Parentage of a rational being means the voluntary co-operation of father and mother with the divine will: nay, it means that the Creator *awaits* their co-operation. What a dignity is this! To think that the great Lord of the universe puts it in the power of man to say *yea* or *nay* to His command, "Increase and multiply." Only in the province of the rational creature do we find this holding good. In the province of the irrational, instinct leads to such functioning as fills earth, sea and sky with organic creatures. When there is a question as to whether the earth is to be tenanted by rational creatures, or heaven peopled by immortal souls, God leaves it to the free will of husband and wife as to whether they will undertake the responsibility. If we dare, with due reverence, put the divine suggestion into words, it would run: "Are you, of your own free will, prepared to co-operate with Me in the peopling of My earthly domain and My Heavenly Kingdom?" Voluntary assent means, naturally, compliance with whatever laws—natural and positive—God has laid down for the absolute wholesomeness of the undertaking.

Looking on marriage as a sacred trust, God-fearing partners will be of one mind in believing that happiness can be theirs only by faithful compliance with all that the laws of God and Holy Church require. The sublime thought that they have been invited to be co-operators with the Creator in bringing His noblest works into the world is well calculated to fill them with awe. It suggests that they bring to that admirable office wholesome and healthy frames, untainted by abuses; that they strive to have their minds well informed regarding their matrimonial and domestic duties; that they live soberly and decently, and that they mutually aspire to the possession of the Heavenly Kingdom to which they are expected to lead their children.

Apart altogether from the legislation of the Church, these are the feelings that spontaneously rise in the human breast, once the dignity of parentage is fully grasped. The Church really does no more than bless and sanction them, by her laws regarding age, liberty, consanguinity, affinity and spiritual relationship: laws which make for health, mutual understanding and morality.

With their outlook transcending the boundaries of time and space—inasmuch as they are called upon to people the Kingdom of Heaven—partners to a marriage should have no trouble whatever in understanding, and in submitting to, the legislation of the Church with regard to unity in the Faith. If their subjection to the Church be a great reality, it must be apparent to them that obedience to her laws is the only safe and sure way to their mutual happiness and the future well-being of their children.

Coming now to the conditions affecting parentage, the mind of the Church is not less clear, nor is her legislation less logical. Even those outside declare that she alone has the courage to raise her voice against that which is, admittedly, an awful modern scandal—the evil of race-suicide. Men of all shades of opinion point to the Church as (in this matter) the savior of society. The mind of the Church is that husband and wife are called by Almighty God to a holy state, and that, in that state, they are subject to the conditions that nature itself insists on. They are perfectly free to exercise moderation; indeed, the Church, in her exhortations before marriage, recommends moderation; but when the rights sanctioned and blessed by God, are exercised, the exercise thereof must be altogether in accordance with the laws of nature. To act otherwise would be to abuse their holy state by a direct contravention of the purpose of God in sanctioning those rights. They are sanctioned primarily for the propagation of the race. Mutual gratification is quite a secondary matter. If mutual gratification be made the *end* of matrimonial matters, in such a way as to impede or frustrate the primary end of this holy union, then God is defrauded of *His* rights, and the unhappy couple fall under His ban.

It requires but little reflection to see that such willful frustration drags human beings down to a level lower than that of the brute creation. In the case of the brute creation, natural instinctive functioning is supplemented by other instincts, provided by the Creator for the weal of the progeny; and, so, animal life is propagated without blight or blemish. In the rational world, they who undertake matrimonial care are expected to exercise reason and faith. Reason is to persuade them that, if nature's laws be tampered with, nature will be revenged. Faith is to convince them that He, who feeds and clothes the birds of the air, will not be less generous in providing for those whose existence depends on the wholesome compliance of parents with His divine will.

The story of the revenge of nature is written large on the pages of modern history. The civilized world now hungers for children, to swell her armies and to plough her fields, but finds, to her dismay, that they come not into the world by Act of Parliament nor at the bidding of wizened theorists. Millions in the world writhe in the agony of nervous and organic diseases, that were unknown to our ancestors. They preferred purse and pleasure to children; now the purse is ignobly emptied and pleasure is no more.

Surely our Catholic manhood and womanhood will not allow themselves to be engulfed in the cesspool of unnatural corruption! Corruption is bad, but unnatural corruption is beyond powers of description. Surely they will enter the married state, determined to accept all its responsibilities and to rejoice when the all-provident God favors them by adding to their riches. And the most enduring riches are those which are created for Eternity—children sent to bless and help parents in time and to rejoice with them, in the bosom of God, forever.

Let the married couple have ever before their minds a high ideal of the honor and the privilege of parentage. It is an act of co-operation with the all-holy Creator; it means adding to the brotherhood of Christ, and augmenting the numbers of those whose souls are to become tabernacles for the indwelling of the Holy Ghost: "Do you not know that you are temples of God and that [His Spirit] dwells in you?"[*] Parentage may mean the propagation of the family name to the uttermost bounds of the earth; the spread of the Faith to nations that sit in darkness; the glorification of the country that holds it most in esteem—for the future of the world will be in the hands of the race that is most faithful to God's law.

But, here, we have less to do with nations than with individuals. Let husbands rise to the splendid level of their manhood, and forswear in the domestic sphere all illegal acts as they would forswear all public robbery. Let wives accept with gratitude and fortitude the burdens that God may lay on them, full of pride and joy that He entrusts them with His creations; that He enables them to present

---

[*] I Cor 3:16

little ones at the Font, to be made His adoptive children. What a stupendous privilege is this! What a triumph of virtue over vice! And how different the results! A neighbor may point to her hoardings as the fruit of her self-imposed sterility, but the Catholic mother can point to the heirs of heaven that enrich her humbler home. When the savings acquired by the childless have been squandered, the children of the fruitful mother will be building up a future for their country and a Kingdom for God.

The consequences of high ideals regarding parentage are simply incalculable. They purify, they ennoble, they lead to virtue, to thrift, to sacrifice and to high endeavor, and they are crowned with joy and honor. Low, vicious and modern views lead to selfishness, narrowness, debility of the body and damnation of the soul.

Catholic parents should nourish deep desires that at least some of the family should dedicate themselves to the service of God, in the sanctuary or the cloister. This is a huge factor in the building up of a virtuous home. It is the secret of the holiness of persecuted Ireland. Even although God should not grant vocations, the very possibility of such is a great incentive to parental virtue. It promotes sobriety, decency, thrift and worthy ambition. It, moreover, strikes a deadly blow at the modern evil we have been combating. To rob Almighty God, *willfully*, of a possible child will be regarded as a pernicious evil, but what will it be to rob Him of a possible priest or nun?

For Catholics, therefore, there need be no hysterical chatter about flag, Empire, etc., with a view to urging them to fulfill their obligations. The thought of the Creative God is, for them, all sufficient. They need no bribes to coax them to keep their pact. They know that when the mightiest empires have crumbled into dust they will be asked by *Heaven's King* for an account of their stewardship. Pointing to their children they will say, "Behold, O God, *Thy* fruits — raised not for empire but for Thy Heavenly Kingdom."

# ELEVEN
## *Motherhood*

FOND remembrance, gratitude and love—no matter how long they may have lain dormant through the benumbing influence of a callous world—are reawakened when, on one's ear, falls the tender word, *mother*.

The word transports us once again to what must ever be, for reverent man, the sanctuary of his highest hopes—his first earthly home. It brings to life again, no matter how long she may have been dead, the gentle woman, who, in that sanctuary, was a very queen—his mother.

Man's wanderings through the spacious world may set him down in places far more fair, may introduce him to women far more gifted, but if he have a heart worthy of the womb in which it first began to beat, he will never, never own, that any mansion, out of heaven, is dearer than the home in which he was cradled; nor will he admit that any woman can be half as tender and true as the one who first gave him sanctuary in her bosom, nursed him at her breasts, taught him by her knee, dragged him—by her watchings and her prayers—more than once from the jaws of death, and, finally, sent him forth for the battle of life encouraged and strengthened by her blessing.

As life goes on it may be his privilege to sit under learned professors; to listen to the eloquence of erudite and saintly preachers; to meet men worthy of honor because of their integrity and their sound common sense; but as he listens he will find himself strangely familiar with the purport of their speech, and well he may, for, years before, the principles evolved by the learned and the saintly were whispered, after a humbler manner, by his own sweet mother.

Is it not this tender reminiscence of home and mother that leads us to hold our breath, and almost to bow with reverence, when a fair young mother appears on the scene, pressing to her bosom the gift that God has given her? How the childless dames in her environment sink into insignificance, no matter what their talents, in the presence of this favored one of God! For here is one who has been faithful to her calling, as a wife, and we rejoice that Heaven has blessed her. We respect her modest blush that outward testimony to the depth of her maternal pride and gratitude. We make way for her, no matter what our personal inconvenience, for we remember that we, too, rested on such a bosom, and we are glad—oh, so glad—to do reverence to one who bears the same title, *Mother!*

Mother! Co-operatrix with the creative God! Nay, after a manner, herself a creator, for her motherly mind is ever planning a bright future for her child, and her nimble fingers are ever at work to secure its fulfillment.

It is marvelous how Providence prepares the way for motherhood. From infancy, all unconsciously, the future mother is learning her lesson. Her doll is the most prized of all her possessions. Around that time-honored idol of the nursery the little girl exercises all the duties of a household, and bestows on it all the care and affection of a mother. In the interests of her doll she is at once mother, nurse, housekeeper and housemaid, school mistress and playmate. In imagination she assists at its birth, sees that it is christened, is solicitous for its education and good breeding, nurses it in sickness, and provides for its amusement on holiday. At one time her doll is preparing for matrimony, at another she is being fitted out for a convent; today she is holding high festival and tomorrow she will be laid out in her shroud. And then there will be a "wake," and a sumptuous funeral to boot. If the child has reached that stage in her catechism which speaks of the Resurrection we may take it for granted that she will secure for her little idol a resurrection most glorious.

Later on in life (it may be said in passing) a special call from God may lead to a surrender of the joys and privileges of motherhood, but the instinct will be there, and, the better it is understood, the more rational, safe and lasting will be the surrender for the greater glory of God. It is as uncanny to surrender, irrevocably, powers that are not understood as to undertake onerous obligations of which one is almost wholly ignorant. If this instinct of motherhood and its probable realization later on in life were sedulously kept before the minds of those responsible for female education, it would be all the better for the moral and physical well-being of the human race. It is painful to see how it is ignored, and still more painful to see that women themselves are the greatest transgressors. If they reasoned, "Every girl is a possible mother," a more decided stand would be taken against irrational dress, violent mannish outdoor sports, and manual labor that involves prolonged fatigue and incessant strain. Serious evils would be prevented in their maturer years if girls and young women had their attention called to the limitations of their nature. No woman, in civilized countries, is likely to be conscripted as an Amazon, but most women, in God's providence, will certainly be called upon to fill the office of mother. They will be healthy and wholesome mothers only on condition of understanding their womanly nature and of applying that knowledge to the judicious care of their health. God infuses the soul, but He looks to the mother to have a becoming habitation ready for that soul in the shape of a healthy body.

From the moment that the Creator blesses a woman with fruitfulness He lays on her an obligation of caring not only for herself but for the child yet unborn. Slowly but surely the little one—bone of her bone and flesh of her flesh—is being matured, and her every movement, in mind and body, will be reflected, for better or for worse, on its impressionable frame. She must strive after great serenity of mind, she must exercise patience and self-control, and be temperate in her habits, otherwise she may transmit hereditary tendencies that will add considerably to the dose of fallen nature that will be the portion of her child when it comes into the world. Many of the evil tendencies with which human beings have to contend owe much of their *virus* to the passions of anger, intemperance or melancholy which dominated the mother during the impressionable months preceding birth. So close is the interdependence of mother and child during that period that no particular knowledge of the influence of heredity is necessary to bring home to the minds of intelligent people the fact that what affects the nervous system of the mother must also affect the child. So much is this the case that it may be safely said, "A patient mother makes a patient child."

If, during the period preceding birth and the succeeding one in which the child is nurtured at her breast, a mother be God-fearing, patient, calm, serene, temperate, clean in mind and body, and orderly in her habits, the child will get a much more wholesome start in life than if the mother were a victim to unruly passions. In sowing, planting, reaping, men do not expect a harvest out of a whirlwind. How, then, can a patient child be evolved if unruly passions are ever agitating the maternal breast?

The primary wish of a Catholic mother is to have her little one made an adoptive child of God at the baptismal Font, to choose reputable godparents, and to bestow a name that will remind her offspring of his or her fellowship with the saints of God. It will be no compliment to the child, and no credit to the mother, to have a name picked out from heathen mythology or from the pages of romance; nor will it lead to the child's comfort, in later years, to have to answer to a name that is likely to provoke the risibility of his neighbors.

Received back from the Font, the mother presses to her bosom a little earthly angel, lent to her by God that she may fashion it after the model of His own Incarnate Son. Oh, what a sacred trust! Who can describe the emotions of a mother in gazing on her own image in the flesh, with the consciousness that the soul within is created in the image of God? For many, many months she lives in a state of rapture, as all of us can see when in going about we are brought face to face with mother and child. Human respect melts away in the furnace of her motherly love. All the world may look on, but her kisses are showered and her fondlings are multiplied without the shadow of a shade of self-consciousness. Scripture is verified in every caress: "Can a mother forget her child?" * God is glorified in every kiss she presses on its brow for she is "glad that a new man is born into the world." †

The mother realizes that the work of training begins with the dawn of intelligence, i.e., when the infant recognizes persons and things outside itself, for, with the dawn, its human nature will assert itself. All educationalists agree that, in infancy, no education can ever surpass that of the mother, who, as someone says, "has the equipment, the leisure and the grace of heart to guide." They admit that the home is the central institution for the upbringing of the young. Whilst allowing the infant all the freedom needed for bodily development, the mother will, nevertheless, in calm yet decided ways, restrain tendencies that make for evil. Its instinctive greed and self-will, which make it clamorous for all that it beholds, will be prudently restrained.

This training to self-renunciation should be carried out as long as the child remains under its mother's care. Self-denial should go hand in hand with consideration for others. The mother should tell the child stories of the value of helping others; she should praise unselfish deeds, and encourage him to help the poor and the weak in his immediate neighborhood. Many, alas, deprived of such training,

---

\* Is 49:15
† Jn 16:21

grow up with deep interest in far-off sufferers but are blind to those who perish in want at their very door.

Children are instinctively greedy about food and sweets, and it is doing them a grave injury not to teach them to restrain their appetites. If those appetites, peculiar to earlier childhood, be unrestrained, there will be little or no inducement to self-mortification when, later on, impure tendencies begin to assert themselves. Accustomed as they have been to gratify every taste, there will be a predisposition to indulge also in those just mentioned. It is also of huge importance to train children to contentment with the food set before them, for, ill otherwise, an insolent and capricious character will be developed.

The mother must not be discouraged by signs of evil in the child. When wicked words—heard by chance—are repeated, the prudent mother, far from checking or reproving the child, will breathe a prayer for its preservation, feeling that reproof would simply impress the words on the child's memory. Silence on her part will lead to forgetfulness. Much the same line of conduct should be followed regarding "rude" acts that are clearly meaningless or mechanical, or, again, not at all habitual. A mother's keen eye will enable her to discern whether such acts are the outcome of accident or design. To pounce upon a child for every *seeming* breach of propriety is to lead to the cultivation either of a wrong conscience or of a hidden and, therefore, dangerous temperament. The buoyancy and naturalness of the child must not be crushed nor frozen. On the contrary, those excellent qualities should be directed into safe channels. The excessive and painful bashfulness of some children is due to unnatural repression.

There is grave danger in too many *"don'ts."* Evil tendencies should be pushed out by putting in good ones.

The feeling of justice is strong in the child, and if he is severely punished for small faults he will be quick to perceive the lack of proportion. He will lose his sense of relative values. Cruel punishment cannot quicken a child's perception. Even grown up people cannot work better when they are in pain. If, by just discipline, motherly love, good example and self-control, you make children happy now, you will make them (according to Sydney Smith) happy twenty years hence by the memory of it. But beware of spoiling them! Children do not like to be spoiled. They *bear* it, but they despise the spoiler.

Although, from its earliest years, the child should be trained to piety, it would be a grave mistake to overburden it. Some of the most worthless men I have ever met were, as little children, dragged off to church, in season and out of season, as attendants on their "pious" mothers. Poor children! No wonder that, in later years, they succumbed to temptation. If, in childhood, *discreet* piety had been seasoned with wholesome play the piety of subsequent years would have been more robust and indescribably more relished.

Some mothers are never content unless their children, in their spare hours, have a "good book" in their hands. By a good book they usually mean one which, even to adults, may be insufferably prosy. By all means let them have good books, of the proper sort, but let them also have access to books of travel and adventure and the stories suitable for their age, otherwise their minds will be stunted and they will grow up most moody Christians. The sturdiest Catholicity is ever to be found where there is most common sense. The commonsense mother is the one who studies her child all round and who, in sweet reasonableness, supplies food for all the powers of the child's soul. Would to God we had more of them!

From this it follows that the questionings of a child are never to be pooh-poohed. They must be attended to. The child must never be told that he "should not put such questions." If the query demand an answer that would not be opportune for his years, the judicious mother, without lying, will easily find an avenue of escape. And even the *semblance* of an answer, so long as it is not contradictory, will satisfy the child for the time being. All progress in life depends on the cultivation of wholesome inquisitiveness. When natural inquisitiveness is rudely and ignorantly repressed, life-long harm is sometimes perpetrated. The child lives to learn that half the world knows all about everything and looks down on the other half that is plunged in ignorance. He curses his fate, for he, too, hungered for useful knowledge, but was only bullied for his pains. Happy the child whose mother encourages him to use his powers of observation; who invites him to put questions and who answers them in season; who trains him to love God's creatures, and to use them as means to know and love the Creator more and more. Happy the teacher into whose hands that child will come in after years. Happy the world, for it will possess a new pioneer in all that contributes to its progress.

Day by day, the mother's splendid work goes on. She presides at morning and evening prayers, sees that grace before and after meals is said; arranges for respectful attendance at Holy Mass and for the devout reception of the Sacraments. She is relentlessly severe with regard to truth, honesty, charity, good manners, cleanliness and order. She abhors the carrying of tales from school, or from the homes of neighbors. She trains her children, boys and girls, to be useful in the house and obliging out of doors. While her attitude fills them with filial fear, she rules by love. And because she loves she is patient, very patient, with their childish defects. And they love, in turn, and prove their love by their ready obedience.

The sensible mother is not displeased with the spontaneous activity of her children, for, gifted as they are with exuberant health, she knows they cannot be everlastingly prim. She is neither suspicious nor mistrustful. When driven to correct her children she restrains herself from anger and over-severity. She does not punish trivial and grave offenses in the same way. She neither bribes nor coaxes, but knows how to dispense praise and rewards in just measure and in due season. She takes care not to confound thoughtlessness with malice, and seldom or never threatens, for she fears to brutalize her loved ones by making them lose their self-respect. She knows, too, that threats, anger and perpetual displeasure breed stubbornness, deceit and lies, and that they build up nasty, shifty characters. She is conscious, moreover, that if her children be *too* much repressed, they will be driven to desperation and that, sooner or later, pent-up energies will burst forth like a volcano.

Such a mother trains her children to be resourceful, to do things on their own account, and not to be ever waiting for a lead. Employment is the best safety-valve for the ever-buoyant child. When everything is done for him and he does nothing for himself, growth of mind and body is impeded. The child should not be cramped; he should be led into the path of self-development and self-education, for he positively hates to have his natural faculties unduly restricted.

The mother never forgets that the moral aim in education is the only *absolute* one and that all other aims are purely relative. Therefore, her first and last appeal is to *duty*, for the glory and the honor of God and the stability of the child's character. She teaches by her upright example, and, therefore, severs herself from those ill-instructed mothers who check, reprove and punish wrong-doing, but are too impatient to train, and too imperfect to give an example of what is good and right.

A time comes when the mother feels that her work is done. But she does not bid good-bye to the world without having many proofs of the efficacy of her training. Sitting serenely in her armchair, with her little stock of books close at hand and the latest newspaper on the table—for the true mother keeps up-to-date—she gives audience to her children and her children's children from far and wide. They come to tell her of the successes that have come through her early lessons. They come to pay their debt of gratitude. They ask her blessing once more, and the blessing seems to them a new birth. And when the armchair becomes vacant, there is no vacancy in their hearts, for mother was enshrined there long ago, and in those hearts she still teaches, soothes, chides, warns against dangers, and blesses. What would the human heart be without its fond, fond memories of a mother? What mother could forbear taking all the pains that are needed to have her memory enshrined for ever in the hearts of those she brought into the world?

# TWELVE
## *Fatherhood*

I SHOULD like to think that all my readers are impressed with the modern anxiety to make something spring from land that, heretofore, was barren. "Allotments" are to be found all over the country. I love to linger near them and to note the efforts of my fellow-men, after their day's work in other places is over. How they weed, and dig, and sow or plant; how eager they look for signs of life, how they coax backward plants, and how triumphant they are when their harvest is, unexpectedly, good. There is a something exhilarating in the cry, "Back to the land." Yes, it is a wholesome cry; it betokens faith and hope. God is behind it all. For if a man sows, it is He alone who can give the increase. The man who tills the soil must find it impossible to listen to the twaddle of him who says there is no God; for, surely, he must be ever in close touch with the Giver of every good gift. From spring unto harvest-time he leans on the Lord. I love to fancy him sowing in the name of God, praying for sunshine or rain as the days pass by, and, eventually, radiant in his thanksgiving.

But there is something that moves me far more deeply. It is the sight of a father, with his little ones around him. If he is a young man, the sight is all the more appealing. Quite unconsciously, his every movement is a new chapter in a most enchanting life. All who run may read. Is this the young man who, but a few years before, was so jaunty and so irresponsible? Is this the individual who was so flippant and so cocksure? The very same, and yet how changed! And changed for the better.

He is now a father, and he bears the impress of the mighty hand of God. He is reverent, he is softened, his horizon is wider; he has a stake in the country, for he has added to its riches; he has a greater right, than formerly, to Heaven's protection, for he has co-operated with the all-creative God. This young father has been chastened in the fire of suffering. Nay, he has agonized! He emerges full of a strange reverence for womankind. The anxieties attendant on childbirth were concealed from him until the moment came when the wife of his bosom was to become a mother. Until then, he had never dreamed of what he had cost his own mother: never imagined that he might have occasioned her death. The hours in which the mother of his own child battled, in a way, with death found him on his knees imploring highest Heaven to befriend her and the yet unborn infant. In that hour visions came to him of what—years ago—had been endured for his own sake, and his mother, living or dead, was revered and prayed for. His mental agony, his hopes, his fears, were almost as poignant as the physical pains of the wife and mother. He united them with hers. He, again, pledged his troth; he regretted any possible unkindness, on his part, in his past; he resolved for the future.

The agony is over. He is told that he is a father. He trembles with joy. He thanks God for His trust. He rises, determined to be worthy of his vocation. He is no longer the wayward youth of yesterday. He is a *man* in very truth: God bless him!

No wonder then that, wherever we meet him, our hearts go out to him. The cynic, the reader of the comic papers, the poor clown whose spare hours are spent in the mimicry of everything that is sacred, cannot understand; but, thanks be to God, it is given to countless numbers to look on the father of a family as a being who must be reckoned with, if all is to go well with the world. For the world is sadly in need of fathers worthy of the name. There would be more, if this sacred theme of matrimony and parentage were not virtually handed over to the scoffer. I have sufficient faith in the goodwill of our young men to believe that, if pains were taken to put before them—in reverent fashion—a few facts regarding the sacred office of fatherhood, they would rise, in splendid style, to the level of their responsibilities. If it be said that nature suggests all that need be known, I am afraid that the statement is not borne out by facts. In bygone days, when the realm of nature was uninvaded by Malthusians and other propagandists of evil, the statement might hold good; but now that the civilized world is overrun by the enemies of Holy Matrimony, it seems to me that prudence demands the relaxation of our traditional reticence. Not that reticence should ever be departed from—God forbid!—but, even as there is a time for silence, so there is a time for speech.[*]
Short of knowing how and when to speak, there is danger

---

[*] See chapter seven.

of moral laxity creeping in, through what is heard in workshops and read in current literature.

What is wanted is clean, plain, straightforward instruction with regard to man's dignity; the functions of that body which God has made the tabernacle of an immortal soul; the conditions necessary for healthy offspring; the reverence and the tenderness due to woman, as wife and mother; the glory that will accrue to God, through the keeping of His laws, and the happiness that will be enjoyed by man, here and hereafter, through observance of these divine laws. The great Creator has confided to man the book of nature for reverent and timely study, and if it be not annotated and commented on by responsible, God-fearing teachers, the enemy of souls will not fail to interpolate to his own liking. Such wholesome instruction—in view of the dangers of the times—would be of immense advantage to young men, destined to be husbands and fathers. As husbands, they would be indescribably more considerate and reverent towards their wives; as fathers, they would be more likely to beget healthy children and more successful in their upbringing.

Let it be fully understood that knowledge, in itself, cannot stem the rushing tide of wrong-doing. So, when we speak of the value of knowledge, it is as an aid to the building up of the moral sense. Humanitarians, today, are advocating knowledge with a view to prevent disease. With us, that is a secondary matter. Catholics welcome knowledge because of the light it throws on God's ordinances—showing them to be wise, just, pure, holy and providential. Reflecting on the attributes of God, thus revealed, our young people will, it is devoutly hoped, be led to embrace the life of virtue, and to abhor the evils that surround them.

My views on the matter may be summed up thus: so long as the mind is unawakened, let it rest in peace, unless a state of life is being embraced in which safe knowledge is of paramount importance. When the mind wakes up and proposes questions, let those questions be answered as fully as is necessary for the immediate needs of the inquirer. And be it noted that these observations apply only to those who have passed the age of puberty. On no account should the child-mind be invaded, short of running risks of bringing on the race a corruption that would exceed the abominations of the cities of old.

These remarks naturally suggest a further question, i.e., to whom are young people to have recourse when their minds are confronted with difficulties arising from what they read or from what they hear? There can be but one answer. God has set up a Teaching Church, to be the sure guide of His children to the end of time. If they are docile listeners to the bishops and priests He has appointed, regular in their frequentation of the Sacraments, prayerful and devout, they will find all their difficulties vanishing. To seek a solution of those difficulties from any merely human source—apart from supernatural helps—or to seek answers to problems from other than authorized teachers, would be to court disaster. At the present time, when platforms are desecrated with discourses on these subjects by incompetent lecturers, and when books and pamphlets are scattered broadcast that awaken, yet never satisfy, curiosity, it behooves our young people to seek whatever knowledge is needed for the guidance of their lives, in the proper quarter. All the knowledge that is needed, in the juncture here alluded to, will be found in the Sacred Tribunal where God dispenses His mercies. All the grace needed to overcome the Devil, the world, and the flesh will be found in uniting their hearts with the Sacred Heart of Jesus in frequent communion.

From the moment that a husband is told that he is something more—that he is a father—his love for his wife should deepen. The child should be a link, binding them more closely to each other, and more closely to the God who in His goodness gave it to them. His kindness, tenderness, sympathy and compassion should grow apace. He should loosen the bonds that, hitherto, bound him down to society outside his own home. He should remember that, in justice and in charity, he is no longer free to roam about with old companions at his own sweet will, nor is he at liberty to indulge in the selfish amusements of his youth. On these points many fathers of families err most egregiously. They live, as before, in clubland. They gad about with the irresponsible chums of former days. They spend their earnings freely, and selfishly, on their own pleasures, in one word, they forget the responsibilities of their new state of life. This is most regrettable. It means the ruin of the home. The mother pines for companionship and finds it not. The children find that father is little less than a lodger in his own home. The father himself is deprived of the sweets of home life, and if, in the earlier days of married life, he ostracizes himself from his own fireside, he will find it almost impossible to relish it as his family increases. I have known more than one family to go to the dogs, simply because the father was hail-fellow-well-met to all outside his own home. All his spare hours were spent outside. He was sober, religious, helpful, popular; courted by priests and people, because of his activities; but a stranger to his home. Who can be surprised at the sad results? A moody, slatternly, heart-broken wife and mother; insolent, reckless, devil-may-care children.

Remembering that he is the head of the house, the father should see to it that from all points of view the mother should be able to point to him as an exemplar. In instructing the children she should be able to refer to father as a model of the virtues she wishes to inculcate; patience, charity, and all the rest. His homecoming, after his day's work, should mean sunshine, gladness, peace and strength. All should be made feel that they can lean on him and that he is, under God, the source of all their happiness. He should be interested in the tasks of his little ones, and in their aspirations as they advance in years. By so doing, he will not only help in developing *their* intelligence (and consequent usefulness in life) but he will, in growing old, retain his freshness of mind, and, so, preserve himself from the deplorable isolation that is sometimes found in old age, not only in the home but in other spheres of life. Who has not witnessed the chasm that sometimes gapes between the aged and the young? At a certain stage, the spirit of inquiry and alertness, on the part of parents and elders, seems to have stopped short, whereas the children have bounded on and have scaled dizzy heights. From those heights they are strongly tempted to look down in scorn on those left behind. It should not be so. A father, even to the end of life, should try to keep alive his enthusiasms; and although he cannot be expected to keep pace with his clever children, he should, at least, ever be within hailing distance—through the active interest he takes in all that concerns their occupations and their aspirations.

Now this can only be verified, in the truest sense, when the father is a man after God's heart. Even more so than when he was an independent youth, the onus lies on him of living an upright life: a life of sobriety, honesty, zeal, patience and charity. He can only persevere in such a life by faithfulness to his duty as a Catholic. He must assist at Mass, frequent the Sacraments, and take a living interest in all that concerns his holy religion. Only thus can he hope to build up a home whose foundations will be lasting: "Unless the Lord build the house, they labor in vain that build it."\* Only thus can he hope to have his name fondly enshrined in the memories of his children until their dying day.

But no matter how excellent may be his own life, the intelligent Catholic can surely see that all will be in vain unless the wife and the mother be of his own Faith. From what has been said about motherhood, marriageable young men will realize that the mother is, after all, the chief agent in forming the child's heart. If the mother be not a Catholic, the father will be almost impotent in training the child for God. This truth should sink deeply into the mind of every youth contemplating Holy Matrimony. Difference in belief means a conflict of ideas from almost every point of view, and the victory is usually scored by the mother, who is always at home, and who has the readiest key to the child's heart. For, in practical life, although the father is head of the house, it is the hand that rocks the cradle that rules it. But the rule is always salutary when the mother is a good Catholic. The father has but to look on, to harmonize with the wishes of the mother, to

---

\* Ps 126:1

smile approval at her holy zeal and to join hands with her in leading the children on and up to God.

# THIRTEEN
*The Case for the Parents*

WE set out with the intention of recovering for the home some of its time-honored prestige. We disavowed the idea of writing exhaustively on the subject, but, all the same, we trust that the youthful readers who have followed us so far will have found sufficient food for thought, and inspiration enough to aid them in forming efficacious resolutions for the future. If the future hold for them a vocation as home-builders, the principles laid down may help them in their efforts. If, on the contrary, that future is to find them, so to speak, on the fence, either as celibates in the sanctuary, the cloister or the busy world, they will, perchance, be led to look on the home with better understanding and with deeper sympathy.

Readers already married, it is to be hoped, will reduce to practice the lessons we have tried to convey; either by improving on their previous good record or by emendating faults that have been brought to their notice. If nothing more had been done in this volume than to bring home to parents the fact that the priests of the One True Church have at heart their temporal as well as their spiritual welfare; that their knowledge of the needs of the home is intimate; that their sympathy is deep, and their compassion profound, it would have been well worthwhile to arrest their attention. For these facts give the lie to many in the world who insinuate that the clergy are a class entirely apart, and that their sympathies are of a purely academic or professional kind. The contrary is the exact truth.

The priest, whose home is now the sanctuary, has recollections of another home—that in which he was nurtured and on which he fondly looks back as the cradle of his purest joys. His vocation, although it has brought joys of a more exalted nature, has neither annihilated nor impaired those which he experienced in the old home. His daily prayer, as he stands at the altar, is for those who were its units—be they alive or dead; he spends himself, in study and in work, that other homes may be made as happy as the one wherein he first saw the light. In this spirit the foregoing chapters have been written and it is in the self-same spirit that the writer now addresses himself to the young men and women who form part of his audience.

If you have been attentive and thoughtful readers you must, by this time, be fully convinced of the urgency of the Fourth Commandment: "Honor thy father and thy mother," for, in spirit, you have followed those revered ones through the long course of their matrimonial life. You have grasped the fact that, though now aged, grey, worn, and maybe broken in spirit, they were once young, ardent ambitious and indomitable as you yourselves are. You have realized that, in ultimate analysis, all their cares, sorrows and trials, all their combats with a cold and heartless world, were borne and confronted for your sake.

Although mutual love brought them at first together, the arrival of their children caused that love to be diffused among them all. It became more and more intense as years passed on and, today, you and the others find yourselves equipped for the battle of life because of the parental love which led a father to toil for you and a mother to spend herself on your behalf.

The study of the preceding chapters must have conveyed more to your minds than can be summarized in the present one. Their contents in formed you of years of labor, self-sacrifice, solicitude, pain and distress all cheerfully endured that you might be thoroughly fitted for the world's work and found worthy to be numbered among the saints of God. If your parents were true to the teachings of their Faith, they acted throughout with supernatural motives, seeking primarily the glory of God and your soul's salvation. By the law of nature they would be more than justified in claiming recompense for all that they have done; but most parents prefer to leave such considerations to the consciences of their children, feeling that they will hearken to the positive law of God, which loudly proclaims that children should honor father and mother. When God speaks so clearly, parents surmise that children, true to their training, will neither be deaf nor indifferent.

It is, therefore, becoming on your part to ask yourselves whether the debt of gratitude has been paid in the past and, if you continue to live under the parental roof, whether it is now being paid. We need not here insist on those obvious explanations of the Fourth Commandment, which are to be found within the covers of your catechism, for we flatter ourselves that, with them, you are perfectly familiar. Faithful to the purpose of the present work we would rather ask if you are sufficiently alive to the part you should play in helping to restore the home to the honored place it held in bygone days. We are, as you know, of opinion that the world must move, but, as it moves, we must guard against the sweeping away of necessary institutions. The home is one of those institutions, and young men and women who live under its roof can do much to preserve it from danger.

Young people should do this by spending a great deal of their free time, in the evening, with their parents, solacing them with their company; by making them sharers in their joys and sorrows; by seeking their approbation in their proposals regarding a state of life, and their sympathy and encouragement in their failures. Much of the happiness of parents is derived from the frankness of their growing sons and daughters, and no outsider can take a keener delight than they in the story of their battlings in the world for position and fortune. Every success scored is proudly and gratefully regarded as, at once, a tribute to their efforts as parents and as a mark of divine favor. Again, could not pleasant evenings be arranged for, as in the days of old? Their charm would more than compensate for the sacrifice made in reducing the number of visits paid to places of amusement outside. Furthermore, not only would the *old* home be cheered by this manifestation of family interest on the part of young men and women, but, through the hours devoted to reading and study, there would be a greater likelihood of the *new* homes becoming all that men could hope for.

We are not blind to the fact that, in many homes, an element of discord may be introduced through the fault of either parent, but in such a case our young people should be slow to judge. They should content themselves by proving kind, patient and sympathetic. They should think of past days in which both parents started life with high hopes and good intentions, and reflect that subsequent failings may be the outcome of hard work, or of mental or physical strain endured for their sake. Let them, moreover, reflect that they are ignorant of the temptations and trials to which their parents have been subjected; let them fear for their own future and, in this humble spirit, show such compassion as, in distress, they themselves would wish to receive.

No young man or woman should be so engrossed with self as to give way to luxurious living—to excessive outlay on dress or pleasure—at the risk of impoverishing parents, or of putting it out of their own power to provide them with comforts as they become old and infirm. In yielding up their earnings, they should remember that they are not in a boarding-house, but in a *home*. Nothing that is given can ever be adequate compensation for all that has been done for them, from birth until they were sent out, fully equipped, into the world. But, over and above the pecuniary help that is given, the gift that will best please God-fearing parents, is the evidence of a virtuous life on the part of each child. Such a life means sustained reverence for parents, union with the other members of the family, obedience to the Church and zeal in the service of God. This zeal would be guaranteed if the time-honored custom of family prayers were honored by observance. Over and above the everlasting reward that is hoped for, such a life brings with it a reward even in this world, for it is written:

"Behold how good and how pleasant it is for brethren to dwell together in unity." *

Unity, in the Catholic home, is to be supported by partaking regularly of the Bread of Life: "He that eats Me the same also shall live by Me." † It is to be cultivated by listening to the Church: "He that hears you hears Me." ‡ It is to be perpetuated in heaven, where the units of the earthly home will know each other if, true to the lessons received from their earliest childhood, they have persevered to the end. In that everlasting home will be found the perfection of the divine gift of love which was the cornerstone of the home on earth. The love of father, mother, brother and sister, will be merged—although not lost—in the love of the Eternal Father, the Divine Son, and the Holy Ghost. Mary, always loved on earth as the spiritual mother of the home, will fill her exalted place in the new home, as Queen and Mother. Saints, numerous as the stars, will give glad welcome to those who, like themselves, were sanctified by the practice of virtue in the earthly home. That home, if its mission is to be fulfilled, must, as we have learned from the preceding chapters, be modeled on the holy home of Nazareth, by unity and fervor in worship; zeal and patience in toil; purity, honesty and sobriety in conduct; resignation in trials and in sorrows; and in supernatural love between parents and children. To build such homes is to build for eternity. May the blessing of God rest on the builders and on all who encourage and help them in their work.

---

\* Ps 132:1
† Jn 6:58
‡ Lk 10:16

## About the Author

Father Alexander was a Franciscan brother and priest. His surname was Murphy and his baptismal name was John. He was born on 23 November 1854 in Greenock, Scotland. He made his first profession in the Order on 5 December 1881 and was ordained priest on 18 December 1886, both in Belgium. He was an active priest of the Franciscan Province in England, serving as Provincial Definitor several times. In addition to this work, he authored *A Spiritiual Retreat, A Mother's Letters, Honour Thy Mother, The Way of Youth, The Third Province,* and *The Method of Giving Missions and Retreats in General Use Among the Franciscan Fathers of the English Province*. He died on 21 August 1941 in Glasgow, Scotland.

*(Information generously provided by the Franciscan Province in England.)*

## *Message from the Publisher*

If you have enjoyed this work, please consider these ways of becoming a patron of our small, family business and helping others come in contact with our publications:

- Purchase copies to donate to a library, school, church, or friend.
- Purchase another one of our publications in the future.
- Purchase copies to sell through your business.
- Donate to our business to help other works come to print.

For further information, visit our website or contact us. We thank you for your patronage.

WORKINGMAN'S PUBLISHING HOUSE
360 East 15th Street, Costa Mesa, CA 92627
www.wphbooks.com
info@wphbooks.com
(949) 205-9736